The Hank's Stories

The Hank's Stories

Hampton Forbes Jr.

authorHOUSE®

AuthorHouse™
1663 Liberty Drive
Bloomington, IN 47403
www.authorhouse.com
Phone: 1-800-839-8640

Published by AuthorHouse   07/05/2012

ISBN: 978-1-4772-2886-9 (sc)
ISBN: 978-1-4772-2885-2 (hc)
ISBN: 978-1-4772-2884-5 (e)

Library of Congress Control Number: 2012911451

DEDICATION

I dedicate this book of stories to my family: my wife, Betty, the love of my life of sixty-three years, and my four children, Hampton III, Deborah, Therressa, and Gwyneth. They stood by me during all these stories.

I married Betty at age sixteen. She was more responsible at sixteen than most thirty-year-old. She birthed our son at age seventeen and our youngest at age twenty-two. If she wanted to do or make something, she read about it (no computer). She had a vast knowledge in various areas from reading and doing. She could furnish the family needs on a minimum budget. She made the children's clothing; for extra money, Betty baked, made draperies, pillow coverings, furniture finishing, upholstery, and flower arrangements, and sold Sarah Coventry jewelry. She was also a lifeguard and swimming instructor. When we moved to Delaware she worked as a hostess, banquet manager, sales service and department manager, antique dealer, run a stove shop business, sold flowers, and managed seven acres, with four in flowers and gardens. She maintained four acres of grass. While working in all these areas she had time for caring for those less fortunate. She is a doer. She is one of a kind; they broke the mold when they made her.

Contents

IN THE BEGINNING was Grandpaw Hinton. I think this is where my stories began. He was a generous, kind granddad. He had a temper that was set off by a small spark. There are a lot of stories about him. He was a big tease, especially if he had a bag of candy. His favorite thing was to thump you on the head. I could write a lot of stories about him, but I will just write two of them.

Granddad owned a farm. One day he was plowing corn with the mule, and the mule was constantly bending down to bite off the young corn. He talked to that mule as if he was a person. He would say, "Don't eat that corn. Your feed is after you have worked for it." Well, that was a hardheaded mule. Granddad warned that mule again. He said, "If you take one more bite of that new corn I'm going to hit you with my fist." I'm sure the mule understood. At the beginning of the next row that mule took a double bite. Granddad got red in the face and came around with a haymaker to the side of that mule's head. The mule got a little wobble in the legs and fell over. Yep, that mule went down for the ten count, only he didn't get up. Granddad had a dead mule on his hands.

When granddad sold the farm he went to work for Westvaco. He lived about three-quarters of a mile from the plant. Grandma would pack a metal dinner bucket with his dinner. It would have a spoon, fork, and whatever glassware was needed to contain his dinner. One day while walking to work the glass and/or the spoon would rattle, a tinkle, tinkle. He would stop and adjust the items in his dinner pail. After a few steps it would tinkle, tinkle again. He repeated his adjustment about three more times. He took off huffing and puffing, no sound. He thought he had it mastered. Then the rattle—tinkle, tinkle—started again. He slammed the dinner pail to the ground and stomped it. He then said, "Now tinkle, tinkle."

Uncle Fred was a great coon hunter he owned good coon hounds; he had a pet coon, Billy he used to train the dogs. He also worked for Westvaco. When getting home from the three to eleven shift he heard the dogs baying on the ridge above the house. He got his .22 rifles and came over to Dad's. He said, "Hamp, the dogs are treed above the house." That's all Dad needed to hear; he loved coon hunting also. They walked to where the dogs were barking. Sure enough, those dogs had a coon treed. Fred was about to shoot the coon. Dad said, "Fred, that might be Billy." Fred replied, "No, Billy is in the cage." He shot, and down went the coon. Those dogs pounced on it and vigorously shook it. When they went by Billy's cage, Dad said, "Fred, Billy has escaped." Yes, Fred shot his pet coon. Make sure you know what you are shooting.

CHAPTER I

Preschool

I AM HANK A DEPRESSION baby, born November 5, 1930, the son of Lucy Hinton Forbes and Hampton Edward Forbes, after whom I was named. Mom was a retired school teacher; she put her children before her job. Dad was a mill worker (foreman in the pulp mill). I had three sisters, who are listed according to age: Lavera Ailice, Dorothy Agnus, and Dreama Arbutis.

We lived on the outskirts of town; our backyard was eight acres joining Hot Springs Mountain. From the front porch the Jackson River could be seen, flowing with clear blue-green virgin waters. This was a child's paradise; it also had a creek flowing from the mountain to the river. (It contained lizards and crawfish.) It was also a retreat for Dad and Mom. They had a garden for vegetables and flowers; also, they had chickens, pigs, and a jersey cow, which supplied us with milk and butter.

Hank stories started at a tender age. I really don't remember this story; however, I will repeat it as I was told. Early one morning Mom bundled me up with blankets and left me warm and serene in the cradle; she gathered her milk container and headed for the barn to milk the cow. I was quite an active child, kicking, tossing, and turning in the crib. When she returned, I was entangled in the blankets, black and blue from lack of oxygen. She survived me never to leave me alone again.

Somehow I was now a special baby (boy).

I remember the next story. I was in a baby gown. It was a hot summer night, and I was in bed with Mom and Dad. I don't know how this got started, I was crying for a corn silk cigarette. I remember Dad getting out of bed and going to the garden for corn silks. I don't remember if the cigarette was lit. I was pacified and went to sleep. This should have been a warning of things to come.

My next story happened at age three. We had a rock wall parallel to the road in front of our house; it had an opening about three feet for a gate. The top surface was eighteen inches wide with a smooth cement cap, perfect for running. I was not allowed on the wall; however, I would sneak on it and just fly. I spent more time looking back for Mom than I did looking forward. Thinking I was getting away with something, I didn't see the gate opening, I glided to a fall on the opposite side. My head and knees were skinned and bruised. Seeing blood, I squalled even louder. The neighbors thought my parents were killing me. Well, no more rock wall for a while.

I was hardly healed when I went under our front porch to play. I loved to play dangerously; I climbed on an old cook stove and jumped off. There was an accumulation of old barrels, hoops, boards, rakes, shovels, and junk around the stove. When I leaped I didn't pick a clear spot; my head hit the shovel, and I fell against other items. I had a muddy face with blood; it looked worst than it seemed. I thought they are going to kill me. Hoping to get sympathy I got up squalling, knowing I would soon get attention. Immediately Mom arrived, panickly. She said, "Hankie, what have you done this time? She carried me to the kitchen and cleaned me up. After removing dirt and blood she discovered cuts between my eyes there were two cuts resembling an airplane. It wasn't bad however I now had something for show and tell. The scar has been with me ever since. Needless to say, under the porch was now off-limits. Just in case I ignored the warning, a lock was placed on the entrance. As I grew in wisdom and understanding, my parents felt I needed to be with children of my own age.

Now being five years old, they enrolled me in kindergarten. It is similar pre-K of today. This is where I learned to play with others without getting hurt. I was introduced to reading, writing, math, and art. I was very good at art. I got a little creative; my masterpiece was the east end of a westbound cat. This got a chuckle from my fans but not from the teacher. That masterpiece and being introduced to the opposite sex was the downfall of my kindergarten career. I was homeschooled until starting the first grade.

Our backyard had a beautiful elongated pool (pond) about two feet deep. It had goldfish, lilies, and floating flowers. It was like a showplace especially when the flowers were in bloom.

I started a new game around the pond. only I knew the game was tippet. I would lure others, especially boys, to get closer to the edge and bend over while watching fish and smelling flowers. This is where the tippet came into play. I would give a quick push on their shoulders and tip them in. This didn't go well with their parents or Dad. My famous words were, "I didn't do it; they just lost their balance." I was broke of this early; Dad gave my brand new stripped railroad coveralls to one of the victims. This is when a fence went around the pond; finally it was filled in to prevent future temptations.

Prior to the pond being filled with dirt, a group of ladies came to admire the pond fish and flowers. Mit was a robust lady, big in stature, who weighed about x pounds. She was leaning over and saying how beautiful it was; one huge flower caught her eye, and she decided to catch its fragrance. She had footing on a rock that tilted. You have never seen such a sight; down she went headfirst, her legs separated and sticking up like the forks in a tree. Mom, being very excited and not knowing what to do, hollered for Forbes (Dad). He came rushing out half dressed and in a tea shirt. Seeing the site he made an about—face and back in the house he went . . . all I could say was, "I didn't do it I was twenty-five feet away as a bystander." The women got together, forcing her legs and thighs down, and finally, after a few bubbles, her head popped up for air. They used a small ladder to assist her to stable ground. When I wanted to gig Dad, I asked him what he saw. He just said, "We don't want to talk about it." I only wish I had a camera. I could have won *America's Funniest Home Vidoes.*

Aunt Garnet lived three houses from our home. I frequently went by for a visit. She was a good cook and often had available pie or cake. I was a little bored this day, and I headed for her house. I pecked on the door, and she invited me in. While sitting behaving myself I noticed a big nickel box of strike-anywhere matches. Aunt Garnet asked me what I wanted. I answered nothing except mom wants to borrow some matches. She gave me a handful and said be careful and go straight home. Well I built a couple small fires on the way home. I struck every match; I now know every possible way to strike a match. I went back to Aunt Garnet's. She came to the door and said, "What is it, Hankie?" I said, "Mom needs more matches." She said, "Hankie what did you do with all those matches?" She said, "You get straight home before I call Lucy (Mom)." Well, she figured me out in a hurry. I went home and took a low profile for the rest of the day. I think Mom knew what I did. Well, a Mom gotta do what a Mom gotta do.

I was such an active boy. I would often wander off like this, especially when Mom was busy and unaware of my intentions. She solved the problem by hiding my clothes and keeping me naked to prevent me from wandering. Well this wasn't any fun at all. It was worse than being locked up. After a few days I decided to break western.

I quietly sneaked out of the house without slamming the door. Off I went to Aunt Dot's house. I don't think anyone saw me; I only passed two other houses. Arriving at Aunt Dot's, I knocked on the door. It was a little chilly; I thought she would never answer the door, but finally she did. With a surprising look she said, "Hankie, what are you doing without clothes?

You are naked as a jaybird. She put a large shirt around me to cover the family jewels. She took me home. Mom, seeing that I was naked, said, "I don't know what I am going to do with that boy."

Mom was having a luncheon for the women of the church. She said, "Hankie, you be a good boy, and when they get here don't say bad words." In the middle of lunch I went in and introduced myself, I then said bad word, bad word, bad word. Everyone laughed; mom didn't think it was funny.

Grandma lived on the corner down from our home. I was still quite a wonder. I decided to sneak off to her place; it started raining harder and harder as I reached her backyard. I began running to the back porch; it was muddy and very slippery. I fell forward face-first, sliding about ten feet and making a crash landing face-first. I made a sudden stop when my head hit cement. Seeing stars and thinking I was dying, I let out a groaning yell that brought the whole family to rescue me. As they reached me I was on my knees, nose and head bleeding, mixed with blood and mud. It was a scary mess. All I could hear was, "Oh, that boy. Call the doctor." After everyone settled down they washed my face and head, splashing alcohol all over my wounds. It was decided I wasn't going to die, so they forgot about the doctor. After the alcohol burned for about ten minutes they walked me home. That walk home was worse than the fall. I didn't know what to expect. Surprisingly, it was okay. Mom said, "Poor little Hankie. He has been hurt again." Well, I had another scar for show and tell.

To keep me closer to home, Dad bought me a new fishing pole. He didn't use a barbed hook; he bent a straight pin to simulate a fishing hook. He baited it up stringing oatmeal on it; that's what we fed the goldfish. He opened the gate to the pond, and I was now fishing. The object of the straight pin was not to hurt the fish but release them unharmed. I became a fishing pro. I think Dad started the first catch and release. Dad was pleased I could finally do something without getting hurt. They gave new privileges, and I could spend time with Grandma.

Grandmaw was house sitting for the Camels while they were on vacation. One day she invited me to go with her. When reaching the property all I could see was toys, toys. It was like Toys "R" Us. I began to play with various toy guns. I especially liked a Roy Rogers handgun. I grew so attached to it that I carried it home with the intention of returning it later. As the days passed I was still playing with the gun. I didn't have a chance to return it. Dad saw the gun. He questioned me of about its whereabouts. I began to tell him of the many toys I discovered while at the Camels' estate. Surprisingly, nothing else was said. The next day Dad said, "I'm going fishing tomorrow morning. Would you like to go?" I replied, "Yes, surely I want to go." We got our gear together. and Dad said, "Pick up the gun you were playing with and bring it along." I thought, "Wow, this is a treat—fishing and playing with the gun. We had no transportation to our fishing spot. As we walked we would pass by the Camels'. Well, big surprise, Dad said, "Take the gun down and tell them you are returning the gun you stole." At this time I wasn't sure whether I wanted to go fishing or not. When answering the door, I quickly announced my presence. I explained about playing with the gun and carrying it home.

The lady of the house said, "Honey, you keep it. Clyde has too many toys anyway. I thanked her but said, "No, thanks. I'm going fishing." Dad had a big smile on his face as I approached, and he slightly rubbed my head. I thought, "Wow, I got out of that one. Mom and Dad were very strict when it came to stealing and lying, I tried to stay on their good side. They are loving and understanding parents.

Somehow I acquired firecrackers, I must have traded something for them. This was a no-no, according to Mom and Dad. They knew I was a bomb ready to explode. I played with them, placing them under tin cans, rocks, and in containers under water, and I practiced lighting them and throwing by hand. I saw a neighbor, Louise, in her front yard. I was getting mischievous and brave. My intent was to get close enough, light the cracker, and surprise her throwing it at her feet. However something went seriously wrong. I lit the firecracker and was slow throwing it. I got the surprise of my life when it exploded in my fingers. It felt as though I was hit with a sledgehammer. Not only that, my ears rang for a week. This you don't try, and if you do, keep it to yourself. Today's troubles are sufficient.

Dad wasn't too strict; however, he didn't believe in allowances. He was one of a kind; he would buy us anything we needed or asked for if within reason. He just didn't hand out money. In other words, no work no money. It was a training that remained with you. I had two areas of work. One was pulling weeds from the garden; it didn't take long, especially if the ground was damp from a rain. Its reward was fifteen cents a row. You picked the row clean of unwanted weeds. Dad would check each row. His comment is, "Anything worth doing is worth doing right." My other job was picking rocks for fifteen cents a pile in the pasture. This wasn't too bad. One day I needed extra money so I decided to make a reduction in the piles, resulting in more piles for a given time period. Dad paid me for each pile. I thought I had pulled one until the next day when he examined my work. I should have known Dad was a follow-up. That was his profession (supervisor); it has more work. I had to equal out each pile to match the sample pile. Again Dad repeated his saying of doing it right. I learned you give a day's work for a day's pay. This has been with me over my employment years.

There was an airport on Mcallister's Hill. It was high above the city of Covington. When I could sneak off I would go there and watch the planes take off and land. Braising I went up to John the pilot and said, "What is it like up there?" He said, "If you have a dollar you can find out." I was fortunate. I had just finished seven piles of rocks. Off we went, I was riding shotgun with a safety belt on. We flew in and out of the clouds; they simulated large cotton balls. Things below looked very small, as if seeing a miniature world. He said, "What do you think?" I said, "This is great. It really is the excitement I had hoped for. What about a dive?" He said, "Are you sure you want to try that?" I agreed, and he handed me a paper bag. I said, "What is this for?" He said, "It's for just in case you get sick (upchuck)." Well, straight up he went; my face felt a little tight. He leveled off and down we went in a swirling motion. We were over two smoke stacks at the Rayon Plant. They looked like they were dancing. He then leveled out. I was a little dizzy, and he said, "Now what do you think?" I just said, "I got my dollar's worth."

I was getting more of an upset stomach. He said, "Are you all right?" "Yes," I replied. "I think I will stay closer to the ground in the future. Mom doesn't need to know about this adventure."

In later years, John and a salesperson were going to the Homestead for dinner and a meeting. The area around the Hot Springs airport was fogged in on the mountain. While trying to find the airport, John undershot the airstrip and crashed on Warm Springs Mountain, killing the two of them.

At the end of our front lot was an alley called the green lane; its name came from foliage, grass growth with poison ivy and grapevines. We often played there; we had horsehoe pits and other sports. On this day no one was in the lane area. The older guys were in the neighbor's yard playing ball. They threw the ball above their head and tried to catch it when coming down. I didn't have a ball. I looked around and found a rock about the size of a tennis ball. I began to pitch it up and catch it on the way down. I gave it more force, sending it higher. I put my arms up in a position to catch it, but the rock came through my hands, hitting me in the mouth. What a lick; my lips were bleeding, and it felt like glass in my mouth. I spat in my hand and teeth particles came out. Now I know they are going to kill me. I went home hollowing for Mom. She said, "What is it now?" I explained the situation as she came toward me. After a glance she said, "I don't believe you; you have ruined yourself for life." They took me to the dentist; he said my teeth would continue to grow until I was twelve. I wore an upside down v in by my upper front teeth. All I want for Christmas is my two front teeth. When I was about twelve the broken area was filled with gold. Now I had two-tone teeth. They stayed with me until I was married, and then I had them repaired with caps. This was while living in Delaware.

Chapter II

Grade School Era

I WENT TO RIVERMONT Grade School. It was about a one and a half mile walk. No one rode a bus; you either walked or your parents were well off enough to afford a car. We didn't get a car until the forties. School was great, and also, you could be a little creative and have more excitement. We didn't change classes; we just went out for recess or physical education. When having a break I would groom my curly hair; my face might be dirty, but my hair was neat. When returning from recess, Jewel, a large, stocky girl who outweighed me by about sixty pounds, would pass my desk and ruffle my hair. This was where she got her kicks, especially when the whole class went into a uproar. Getting very uptight, I would hold my temper and give her a special smile. My wheels were turning. How could I get even with her without being near. I slept on it; the next morning I had the answer. I got a roofing nail left over from one of Dad's jobs; it was about one and a half inches in length. It stood upright due to the large head. I arrived early that morning and placed the nail in a position to catch the weight of her thigh. As she came in, I was seated. She passed by and smacked me with an upward swing to the back of my head, and then she giggled. I didn't even look up; she flopped down in her seat and came up like a flopping chicken and squalling like a panther. She looked at her seat to see what it was. While standing, her dress was creased and humped in the vicinity where the nail pierced her rear. The class erupted; I kept my cool, however. The teacher said, "Mr Forbes, go to the office." My famous words were, "I didn't do it." They couldn't convict me. I volunteered no information; no one saw me place the tack, and I wasn't near her when the excitement began. I think she got the message—, don't mess with the hair.

At Rivermont School, I was attracted to girls and vice versa. Daisy was a girl I kidded with; she was in by class. We spent our spare time together. She was a tall, lanky blond; her legs were extremely long, especially for a girl. She was a head taller than I was. The class was out for recess. She began rough housing me, punching arms, legs, and body, also messing up my hair. She gave me a goose egg on my arm. That was enough; I caught her ponytail and gave it a backward pull—big mistake. The chase was on. I was ahead of her, but she, with those long legs, began to catch up. I knew if she caught me I was going to get hurt. As she got in reach of me, we both were flying. I suddenly, without warning, dropped to my knees and ducked. With her momentum out of control, she flipped like a wagon wheel, legs and arms rotating like spokes. She got up with a little help from her friends. When she became a little more stable she said, "You little—. I will get you later!" From then on I needed eyes in front and back; I knew somehow it wasn't over. Later on we called a truce, I was happy for that.

The river was just below our house. It was a virgin stream and was crystal clear. This was a great summer hangout; we called the swimming hole the rock pile because of the many small and large rocks. My sisters, Lauver and Dorothy, often went with me to this area. After fooling with me, teaching me to dog paddle, they decided to cross to the other side and go downriver to another swimming area. They swam safely through the deep area to the shallows on the other side. Being a novice, I waded until the water was over my head and then I began to swim to safety. After about thirty minutes I was tired and decided to go back to the other side. That was a big mistake I started swimming in the shallows; when I reached the middle of the deeper water I was out of breath. Suddenly, I began to sink. I was numb, seeing stars and flashes of light, I knew I had to do something. Being good at swimming underwater, I began the underwater swim, catching onto bigger rocks and pulling myself to safety. Finally I made it. Shivering, shaking, and out of breath, I had made it. I know the light was an angel at my side. This was a lesson well learned: stay out of deep water until you have mastered swimming. This is something else I didn't share with Mom and Dad. The river would become off-limits.

Grandmaw moved to another location; it was close to an active stream. The front and back yards were level, a safer environment in which to play.

Mom and I went down for a visit; it was about a mile from our house. On this day they let me explore the front and back yards. Being adventurous, I decided to explore beyond the property boundary. I found myself admiring the rolling waters of the nearby stream. On the bank edge I noticed a group of bottles piled up. Neighbors would pile unwanted items by the stream, and when high water came it would wash the things away. Seeing all those bottles, I decided to create a game. I would throw large bottles in, and as they floated away I would throw smaller bottles, trying to hit or break the floating ones. Well, if it could happen, it would with me. I picked up a partly filled bottle and drew back to throw; the solution in the bottle went all over my head, shoulders, and body. Within a minute I had a burning sensation around my head, ears, and neck. Luckily, nothing was in the area of my eyes. Again I went squalling for help. When I got to grandmaw's she immediately saw the problem, my clothing were being diluted. She stripped me naked, rinsed me down, and gave me a sponge bath with vinegar all over. The vinegar neutralized the acid. Thanks to the wisdom of the older generation, Grandmaw saved the day.

I was still having problems playing alone; Mom and Dad decided I could have friends again. I had a friend called Dickey, who lived in the corner house over from us. We did a lot of things without accidents. On this day we ventured from our backyard toward the edge of the mountain, where there was a stream. Looking for excitement, we rolled rocks down the bank into the water; this went well until we turned over a big flat rock. As it began to slide down the embankment, it disturbed a nest of yellow jackets. We couldn't outrun them; while we were hightailing for home they like to eat us up (stinging) as we ran. Mom heard our cries and met us as we entered the back porch; she had a broom and beat the bees from us. I don't know which was worse, the bee stings or the broom whipping. Mom removed our coveralls to eliminate the bees. Wow, that was a relief. We had welts all over; this type of bee stings and bites at the same time. What will be will be. I seem to invent accidents.

I decided to spend a quiet day at home and try to be a good boy. I helped Mom do some minor chores. While taking a break I watched her washing clothes. It was neat watching the agitator swish back and forth. The most exciting was the way the clothes went through the wringer and came out flat with less water. After evaluating this procedure, I thought and thought. Then I decided to see what the wringer would do if I inserted my fingers—big surprise. The first thing I knew, my arm was in the wringer up to my elbow. As I moaned, Mom saw the problem. She hit a lever that disengaged the ringer. We had a lot of excitement that day. In those days you could call the doctor and get home service. The old doctor said, "You are lucky—no broken bones and no damage to your elbow." He said when leaving, "Keep your hands in your pockets."

It seems the harder I try to prevent accidents, the more I create. On this day I was going to help Mom.

Everything was usable; people saved meat scraps, lard, oils and other fatty materials. They had a formula using lye. When cooking, these ingredients would create soap, called lye soap. It was cooked in a cast iron kettle, was allowed to cool, and was sliced into square cakes. This may involve three families; the soap was divided and placed in baskets. My cousin and I were asked to carry the basket containing the soap to our basement. As we made our way home, only two hundred yards, we heard shots in the close distance. As we walked from behind the garages we heard more shots. Suddenly I had a harsh stinging in my right arm at the elbow area. I dropped the basket, looked at my arm, and saw blood. My shirt also had a hole in it. Glenn hollered for help and also, "Stop shooting." The shooting stopped, and Mom came running. She was shaking her fist in the direction where the shooters were. She said, "I knew something like this would happen if this shooting was allowed." She immediately applied pressure to the wound area and using a scarf applied pressure above the wound. I was taken to the hospital. When they x-rayed my arm, I could see the bullet. The purpose of the x ray was to ensure that the bullet hadn't glanced to another location. I was given ether when the bullet was taken out. The entrance area only made a small scar; it seemed I was compounding show and tell stories.

Bobby, one of my friends, and I decided to do something where there would be no danger. We figured out how we could get cigars and smoke up a storm. I went to the filling station at the top of the hill. I said H. E. Forbes wants two cigars. I wasn't telling a lie I was HEF Jr. They gave me two cigars and said that will be a nickel. (I don't remember taxes). Off to the riverbank we went, each having a cigar. We wet it around, lit it up, and the smoke rolled.

Things seemed fine for a couple minutes, but then my head began to spin. Dizzy, I was. The more I looked at the flowing water, the sicker I got. Bobby wasn't feeling so bad; he was used to smoking. This was the end of cigars for me.

My uncle Lawrence needed some interior painting help. Dad and two others were painting; they were having a blast, telling jokes on each other. I guess the gallon of wine they were sipping accounted for some of the laughter. Seeing they were so happy, being tempted, I decided to take a sip or two. It made me a little dizzy. After taking another swig, my stomach began to ache. I needed to go to the bathroom. They were painting in the vicinity of the bath area. I had to go in a big way. I staggered out to the creek, got under the bridge, and relieved myself. My clothes were off and were all tangled up; I couldn't get them back on. Finally I managed to get back to where the painting was taking place. Dad saw me and said, "What the heck are you up to?" Well, I at least wiped with my shirt. Dad was a little furious. He cleaned up his painting tools, and home we went. Dad and I both were in trouble. I think Mom gave Dad the worst talking-to; I bet he won't let that happen again.

This is a sad story. I thought seriously about not including it; however, this is a part of my life, and it has had an effect on me ever since.

This is about Bob Stanley, Jackie, and me. We went to Rivermont School. We were in different classes (grades). Bob Stanley and Jackie went half days; I was a little older and went the full day. It was a mile to Bob Stanley's house, half a mile to Jackie's, and over a mile to my home. At noon I was going home for lunch. Bob and Jackie were off for the day. The three of us were walking toward our homes. Jackie was almost home; he was at his driveway. Bob had about one quarter of a mile to his house; I had one half of a mile to home. We were walking side by side. As we approached a parked car on our side, we stopped for a second. The car was cranking but wasn't starting. I walked around the car just about fifty feet. I stopped for some reason and looked back. The other boys were still waiting; the car finally pulled out into the road to go the opposite direction. It stalled in the middle, blocking traffic in both directions. Suddenly a car came down the hill traveling in our direction. Rather than hit the stalled car, it swerved to the right. It picked off (hit) Bob, ran over him, and threw him into the store steps. Jackie was still standing there, and I ran back not knowing what I was going to encounter. Bob was lying there face up and bleeding from his head, nose, and mouth. The driver excitedly lifted Bob's shoulders up. His scalp fell over his face. I shouted, "You have killed him." I think Jackie went on home.

(I often wondered, "What if I had taken him around the stalled car with me?")Shook up, I started toward home. At about one hundred yards away, I met his mother with her apron on, running in that direction. She asked, "Hankie, what has happened?" I just couldn't answer. I went home for lunch and returned to school. In those days there were no canceling classes. Something like this you don't forget. I ended up on nerve pills. Was this encounter the reason?

Mom and Dad seldom left us home alone (they must have had a reason). On this occasion I thought it would be much safer staying home with my sisters. I was trying my best not to get into trouble. I don't remember what I did to Laver, but she locked me out of the house. I knocked on the door, but she refused to open it. She placed her face against the front door glass, made a face, and stuck out her tongue. In a mad fury I hit the glass with my fist and broke it out. Now I knew I was in trouble. This wouldn't have happened if Mom had been there. Since I was barred from the house, I went down to the store. I was bragging about what I had done, getting even with my sisters, not knowing Dad was behind me hearing the whole story. Well, home I went by the ear. Mom said, "Forbes, those girls have been picking on Hankie again." Mom felt we were all guilty; if you punish one you punish all. Besides that, she said, "If we were at home this wouldn't have happened." Needless to say, I think Dad was happy with the decision. He repaired the glass; however, he said, "Next time you will pay for the replacement."

Fishing was one of my favorite activities. On this occasion I got my fishing gear together, including a bait can filled with lizards. I headed for the river just below the house. I entered the river and waded across to the shallows. I stopped for five minutes to catch additional bait. I started fishing about one hundred yards upstream from the rock pile. I began catching fish immediately; they were biting lizards. Trying to catch bigger fish, I changed bait for the deeper water; this is where the larger fish were. Up to this point I had caught seven sun perch and redeyes (rock bass), and one fall fish—they are similar to a saltwater tarpon. Then I caught one bass, about fourteen inches long. I waded through a rocky area. Stepping between two rocks, I stepped on a broken bottle with a sharp spear, sticking it into my foot under the big toe. It was a bad cut; it burned as water opened the wound. I held the area closed and made it to the bank. The next thing I knew, I was being stitched up at the doctor's office. Here was a lesson to be learned: wear shoes.

Two months later I could feel a burning and stinging sensation when adding pressure to the area (walking). The side of my big toe had a reddish swelling effect and was very painful. A piece of glass was broken off within my foot. Finally the glass worked upward and out on the side of my big toe. I was now wearing some protection. I was two months without fishing; this was worse than the cut.

While my fishing privileges were taken, I decided to start fish bait sales. I was good at catching lizards; the creek behind the house was my source of bait. We had about one-half mile to make our catch. After harvesting dozens of lizards, I noticed a large number of crawfish. I had a separate container and began to catch them also. Lizards were sold by the dozen in sizes small, medium, and large. The starting price was thirty-five cents. The word got around, and I had more customers than I needed. It was confining; I had to take care of customers. At times I would wholesale the bait to other dealers. Just to get a break this seemed to be a safe job, until one day I got into a lot of lizards. Getting a little reckless, I placed my feet on each side of a big rock where lizards were running. Gently raising the rock about ninety degrees, to my surprise a big snake was coiled, ready to strike any moving object. My feet and legs were the targets. Gently I lowered the rock without an incident. I got my bait can and went home without looking back.

Another day was catching toads; this was on dry land and seemed much safer. After catching six toads under rotten logs, I rolled another log over. Wow, what a surprise. I heard a buzzing sound, and the area smelled like cucumbers. The underside of the log had a den of rattlesnakes. I almost crapped; by gins, this is a dangerous business. With my luck I could be a casualty. I think I will stick to fishing. I put a sign up out front: Out of Business.

As I grew up, bicycles became a way of transportation—a lot faster than walking. When there was only one bike, we rode double. On this occasion Elwood was the driver, and I was sitting on the crossbar. We started down a steep grade toward town. Robert and Bruster were walking in the same direction on the side of the road. As we picked up speed I told Elwood to get as close to them as possible. As we approached I stuck out my arm with a clinched fist. I hit Bruster in the back of the head; he turned a double flip. By the time he recovered we were long gone. I looked back. Bruster was staggering to his feet, looking back to see what caught him from behind. Luckily I didn't break my arm or wrist. The joke was, "Did you see where it came from?"

While hunting behind our house, I walked several miles. I wasn't having any luck, I saw squirrels, but they were too far to shoot with my Remington 16-gauge automatic shotgun. Finally I sat down to rest, and, to my surprise, I scored on two. I saw one just as it entered into a hole in a hollow tree. I just waited him out; finally he came out and sat on a limb scratching himself. At that point I raised the gun, aimed, and fired. He hit the ground with a thud; quietly I went over and picked up my kill. While standing there for a minute I heard a scratching noise close by. I listened and waited patiently. The sound got closer and closer. I wasn't afraid; I had the gun. Suddenly a turkey was feeding in the ravine. When it looked down, quietly I raised my gun, took aim, and fired a good shot. It flopped around. I started home with the game, and when I got to our property I spotted a squirrel going into a hole at the bottom of a hollow tree. I decided to smoke him out. I built a small fire at the bottom of the tree and threw some grass on it. The smoke began to roll. I waited patiently for the animal to come out. As time passed, two flying squirrels came out and landed on another tree. It was getting late. I put the fire out and headed home. To my surprise, two days later the tree was burning on the interior hollow area. I went back to the tree, started another fire, wet down some papers, and created a steam-like cloud. The steam from the wet paper put out the fire on the tree interior. Steam is 212 degrees; fire won't kindle at that temperature. This was my lucky day; I didn't set the woods on fire.

This day my luck ran out. The upper part of Westvaco was known as the wood yard; it was a storage area for pulpwood. C& O engines called shifters would daily bring pulpwood and other materials in and remove the empty boxcars.

Dad had often warned me to stay away from the boxcars and to stay away from the tracks. There was no warnings when the shifters might move, coming or going. There was no set schedule; this was a dangerous area. I was at the rock pile (swimming hole), and I decided to go home. Seeing the boxcar in a stationary position, I decided to climb up and run on the walkway of the cars. My dad was on his way to work and caught me at my worst. I climbed down the boxcar on the opposite side, hoping Dad would go on by. I crawled under the car to the other side of the track, and, to my surprise, Dad was looking down on me. He was shaking a limber switch and giving me a safety lecture. His voice was very nervous. He said, "What have I told, boy? Do you want the train to run over you?" He led me from the area across the road to the lane going to our house, I had on short pants. He had cooled down a little; however, he switched my legs for the first time. Usually he would just take my hunting and fishing privileges. As I proceeded home I noticed long welts on my legs. When I got home I was still sniffing. Mom said, "Who did this?" She was furious; I didn't tell her the reason for the punishment but just that dad did it. My dad got off work and was home by eleven thirty. Mom waited up for him. The next morning Dad woke me and said, "I am sorry."

To get on my good side Dad said, "How would you like to go fishing today?" Well, everything was forgotten. I couldn't wait until I got my pole and tackle. We got into the station wagon; on our way Dad explained the dangers of being around moving trains. I realized it was for my own good.

We caught several fish and had a lot of bites. We were running out of bait. Discussing it with Dad for approval, I decided to walk down the river bank, catching toads along the way. I walked through a briar patch with berry vines and thorns; they were picking on my jeans. I felt a little scratch. It began to itch. When I got back to Dad's location I began to rub the area. The itching worsened. Pulling up my pants leg, Dad noticed two dots about an eighth of an inch apart. He examined it. Immediately he said, "You have been snakebit."

We went to the doctor; he examined the area and said it was a surface bite. The majority of the venom went in my trousers, not a vein or deep flesh. It was too late for suction to work. The poison had dispersed into the area of the swelling. He gave me an antibiotic and told me to keep an eye on the swelling and call him if it worsened. The next morning there was little swelling; it had a reddish blister the size of a silver dollar. The venom had taken its toll and deteriorated an area about one quarter-inch deep. As time passed it had an odor. I was treated with a stronger drug. It healed within a month; however, it was a smooth reddish scar with no hairs in that area. Later I came within two feet of another poisonous snake, and the area of the bite broke out into a huge blister from the fumes of the snake. I learned it isn't the snake you see, it's the one you don't see that bites you.

Mining iron ore was a business started in the twenties The ore was taken to the furnaces, where the rocks were melted and the iron was retrieved. One mining area was in a dry-run hollow, the remains of a dug cave, from which ore was mined. It was located on the face of a ridge. The entrance was small, due to the entrance being closed and then reopened by animals or people. It was made passable for entering. Inside, it had various rooms where ore was removed; the back end of the cave had an upper level. We carried in a tire and other materials and set the tire on fire at the upper level. It burned with a beautiful flame with various colors; it lit up the entire cave.

Flashlights or candles were needed. After a while the flame flickered, puffed, and went out—total darkness. It then flickered and began to burn as air blew into the cave. I realized the fire was depleting the oxygen in the cave. We took this as a warning and ran to the surface. It was another angel looking out for us; we were fortunate that we weren't suffocated. I hope we learn from our mistakes.

During the Second World War, Westvaco made a laminated waterproof paper with tar. It was used for military packaging. The reject edge rolls were taken to the dump. We would pick up the three-inch-wide rolls and use them for building campfires. On this occasion, Jackie and I were inside the cave. Richard was on the outside. He decided to play a trick on us by filling the cave entrance with the flammable strips taken from the rolls and setting it on fire. When I saw the flames inside the cave, I thought about the oxygen being depleted when the tire was burning. If we stayed inside the cave we could die. I said to Jackie, "Hold on to my belt. Run and don't stop until we pass through the fire and are outside." As we ran through the flames we were burned around our head and face—hair and eyebrows singed. Our clothes protected our bodies. When we were outside overcoming the smoke and excitement, we looked for Richard. He was nowhere to be found. He had hightailed it out of our sight. He kept a low profile until we got over the event. Needless to say, this was my last visit to the cave. The opening was filled in again by unknown persons.

I love sports such as hunting, fishing, and camping—just being in the forest and enjoying all of God's creations. My friends Jackie, Sonny, Glenn, and I often go to the head of a small spring stream in the George Washington National Forest, about three miles up the mountain behind our house. We camp at this area because of the availability of water. (It amazes me how water comes out of the ground from a higher level, then seeks a lower level, and ends up back at the same starting place.) Because of the spring, this area has abundant wildlife—deer, turkey, squirrels, fox, coons, and a variety of birds. We cook over an open fire; bacon is placed on a green branch and placed above the flames. Soup and meats are cooked in an open can. There's a trick to cooking eggs. We add water to a paper cup, place the egg in, and set it in the fire coals. The water boils in the cup; it doesn't catch fire because the water keeps the cup at 212 degrees. Paper won't burn at this kindling temperature. We have a problem transporting eggs; they either crack or burst. I had the bright idea of cracking the eggs and placing them in a sealed jar. We did this on our next trip.

We prepared everything for a weekend outing, packed our gear, and started up the mountain about one o'clock. We arrived at the campsite about four in the afternoon. We built a fire nd started our meal. After eating, we told a few stories, including some Hank stories. We got in our sleeping bags and listened to the animals of the forest until going off and on to sleep.

In the morning we were up at dawn. I couldn't wait to try the eggs. The bacon was cooking, and the potatoes were in the coals. I wiped out the frying pan, placed a little butter in it, and proceeded to open the jar with the eggs. There was a pressure-hissing sound. Wow, what a surprise. The eggs were spoiled (rotten). They had a sulphur smell similar to the paper mill. I tried to figure this out. I guess the eggs were sealed in their shells but not good enough in a jar. I guess I won't try this again.

Hen was an assistant game warden; he was a friend and neighbor. He lived at the end of Dad's front property; he was also building a home in a small ridge.

We were at the campsite early morning, feeling our oats, having a water battle. We had ganged up on Sonny and chased him from the site. Sonny came sneaking back, saying Hen is behind you. We thought he was kidding and wet him again. Suddenly, there was the smiling face of Hen; he thought he would catch us hunting. He said, "What are you boys doing? What have you killed?" He searched our gear, looking for a gun. He wasn't happy walking three miles for nothing. He wrote each of us a summons for having a fire without a permit.

On the day set for court, Hen's superior talked to me about confessing the intent to hunting, and the judge would go easier on us. I nodded as if to agree. In court we pleaded guilty of not having a fire permit. But hunting we were not. The judge looked at Hen and the warden and said, "I see no wrong in what these youngsters have done. It is better for them to be in the forest on a Saturday night than hanging around some street corner or joint. Then he said to us, "The next time you go camping, stop by the forester's office and get a fire permit. We were happy with this decision; however, Hen was on our minds. How do you get even with a game warden? (Then I had an idea.)

Remember the house he was building on the mountain ridge?

We were still thinking how Hen tried to railroad us. The following day we went up the mountain to where Hen was building his house. It was on a high ridge and had a beautiful view of the river and surrounding mountains. Another friend, Bobby, who lived next to Hen, joined us. The new construction had no bathroom installed at that time. An outbuilding sat on the edge of a cliff. It was a two-seater outhouse (toilet). We had our eyes on it. It would tip over with a little help. While Bobby was inside relieving himself, I placed a rock about a foot back from one corner. With the help of others, I found a strong chestnut pole and placed it over the rock and under the corner. We all pushed down on the pole; the john house started to rock. Bobby was trying to open the door as we continued pushing. Just before the climax, Bobby rolled out the door, pants down to his knees, as the john house went over the cliff. When it hit a lower level, it exploded into about five pieces. Bobby was saying words and scrambling to get his pants up; he wasn't too happy with us. However, he agreed this was a good payback for the way Hen treated his neighbors. I guess you would call this revenge.

Dad had planned to work on the hunting camp. Dad and ten others had the hunting camp on Back Creek Mountain. It was about three miles off the main road. It sat in a flat, clear area with one hundred acres of rolling hills and timber. It was made with locust logs and was chinked with mud. It had a dirt floor, kitchen, two stoves, and bunks to accommodate eleven-plus hunters. The tar paper roof was cracking, shrinking, and causing a leak.

On this day Dad said to Mom, "I am going to take Hank with me to repair the camp roof. It will be a fun outing for him; he loves the woods." Mom said, "Don't let him get hurt."

Others were involved. All were busy sweeping the roof and heating the tar over an open fire. They were carrying the tar in a bucket up the ladder onto the roof. They had a flat broom for smoothing the tar. I decided to give them a break and filled a bucket about two-thirds full. Up the ladder I went. When trying to transport from the ladder to the roof (you guessed it) the bucket upset on my chest. I had tar from my shoulders to my shoes. I was hoping for sympathy. Uncle Henry said, "Hamp, I told you to leave that boy home." Well, Dad wasn't too happy with me or the comment. We found a pair of oversize pants; the rest of the tar was cleaned with kerosene. I thought, "I hope no one lights a match." Mom got a little uptight when I arrived looking like a hobo; she gave me a thorough examination and bath.

While going to Rivermont School, I read about applying pressure to someone's chest and it would put them to sleep (pass out). Well, being curious, I wondered if this would happen. I explained the theory to Robert, a classmate. He said, "Why don't we give it a try? I will be the guinea pig. A group of boys were standing around waiting to see the results; at this time we were all late for class. I stood behind Robert. I told him, "Hold your breath for a while, and I will put my arms around your chest and apply pressure." I placed my arms in position and began to squeeze. I did this for about two minutes. He didn't feel limp, so I thought it had failed. I let Robert go. He hit the floor with a "plump," headfirst, putting a goose egg on his forehead. I sprinkled water on his head; everyone scattered out of the restroom then. I thought, "This is not going to be a secret." After the water hit his face he began to moan. They took him to the infirmary and me to the office. My punishment was one week in study hall after school with no unsupervised bathroom visits. I was limited to one visit to the bathroom a day. I was lucky no letter was sent home. Mom never knew.

Mom had a cow that provided milk and butter for our family. Our pasture was small, and the grass was limited. For better and more pasture, the cow was walked one half mile on the highway to another location. One of my choirs was to walk with the cow to and from this area. On this occasion I was late starting home with the cow; it was getting dark. I had a flashlight I shined on the ground to be seen by oncoming traffic. A car came around the curve, swerving and crossed to our side. I flipped the light as the car crossed into the gravel and hit the cow with a side glancing blow. I was scared to death; blood splattered all over me. The car hit and ran without stopping. I went to check on the cow lying in the ditch; she wasn't dead. I ran home; I didn't know how I would explain this. Reaching home I just said, "Come quick. The cow has been hit by a car." Mom said, "Are you all right?" "Yes," I replied, "just shook up." Mom and Dad checked on the cow. She was beyond saving; she had a long cut on her side plus internal injuries. The cow was butchered, and the meat was processed by canning. Thanks to God I wasn't injured. Needless to say, we didn't have a cow for a while.

Things were kind of boring—the same ole, same ole. Jackie and I thought it would be adventurous to take a trip (run away). We saved our money, planning a Florida trip. When totaling our savings, we were short on finances. We decided to go ahead with our plans; we could work as we traveled. We walked to Route 220 and began to thumb. We caught a ride to the next town. We began walking again about two miles to Route 220. We thumbed for a while with no rides. We are getting nowhere; we saw a Greyhound bus coming our direction. It was time to change plans. We flagged the driver; he went by us about twenty-five yards before stopping. We caught up to him and hopped aboard. We asked, "What is the fare to Roanoke?" I don't remember the fare, but we paid it and were on our way to the big time. After arriving in Roanoke we found our way to Route 220 South. We thumbed until dark, hoping to get a ride. I guess people are cautious about kids thumbing. We were hungry and a little scared. We walked to a location where we bought drinks and Nabs. Then we were troubled about where to find a safe sleeping place. The air was getting cooler; we had limited clothing. The park looked safe. It had benches and plenty of lights. We slept on a bench and woke early the next morning, hungry and still sleepy. We wandered upon a small restaurant, where we ordered egg sandwiches and milk. This satisfied us for a time.

As we were exploring the city a lady approached us; she looked like someone having authority. I was a little nervous not knowing what to expect. She said with a firm voice, "Why aren't you boys in school?" Jackie looked at me with fear on his face and said nothing; he was waiting for me to answer. I said, "We are from out of town shopping with our parents." Seeing we were not skipping the city school, this statement (lie) seemed to satisfy the truant officer.

While in the city we found a junkyard with all kinds of salvaged cars and vans. We searched through and found one that the windows and doors worked, and the door locks worked. The seats front and back were comfortable for sleeping. I thought, "Is this what I traded my nice bed at home for?" Well, it served the purpose; the nights were getting cooler. We walked back and forth to Route 220 daily without getting a ride.

We finally gave up on our adventurous journey.

We walked around the outskirts of the city and found a dairy processing plant. There was a barn-like shed for housing bales of straw nearby. This would be ideal for our next quarters. We noticed the milk drivers returning from their daily routes. Walking around the area one of them said, "What are you boys looking for?" I replied that we needed a job. He said, "I can use one of you. Can you be here at four in the morning?" I'm not a morning person, but I agreed. We slept in the barn between bales of hay. Various sounds woke us up, but the shelter was quite comfortable. We woke up during the early morning with traffic sounds. Again I thought about home, mom and dad, clean clothing, food, warmth, and a bed. Before leaving, I told Jackie to go get something to eat, stay close, and return to the shelter. I also said, "I will work at the job and see just what is involved." The driver was very nice; after loading the truck, he suggested breakfast on one of his stops. I was all for that—wow, eggs, bacon, milk, and a doughnut. I tried not to eat it as if starving. It was actually a fun job filling orders and meeting people. He also gave me chocolate milk blended with double cream. This, again, was a treat. He kept a book on sales. It had to balance between starting and ending inventory; somehow he included the milk we drank. The next day was a duplication of the first. At the end of the second day, I ask if one of his friends could use Jackie. He said, "Bring him with you in the morning; we will work out something." That evening it was windy and blowing snow. We went out to get something to eat before retiring for the night. As I noticed Jackie in the light, he was real messy. He reminded me of a roughed up coon, having black around his eyes and neck. We went to a bathroom, where he cleaned himself up. I also washed up. I began to think about the snow, and home. I had a rabbit, and it was due time for her to birth. I sent a postcard home, saying we were okay, but to make sure the mother rabbit was in a warm box. Getting this message, Mom and Dad made a trip to Roanoke. Disappointed in not finding us, they reported us missing and returned home. The next morning as we headed for work we noticed snow in the mountains. We completed the day's work about noon. It was getting colder, and we discussed returning home. We had enough money for bus fare, and home we went. At home I was greeted with love, similar to the parable of the prodigal, or lost, son. There was no negative conversation. Mom made my favorite cakes, pies, and food. I don't know why I did such a dumb thing. My mom and dad loved me, and I wanted for nothing. There is no place like mom and dad and h-o-m-e.

I would advise anyone never to do this; it is now more dangerous. You could be kidnapped or worse.

Summer and fall were ending; winter was here. It wasn't much fun—cold, snow, and ice.

It was a Sunday morning; we all dressed in our finest and went to a little church in the village. After church I asked if I could hang out with the older guys. "Okay," Mom said, but don't go far, and don't get hurt." We all went to the river, which was iced over in the smooth water and was only frozen about four feet in on the fast-water edges. After skating on the river, the big guys decided to walk the ice about two miles up the river. I wasn't too keen on this. Mom said don't go far. After some persuading I tagged along behind. As we advanced up the river I was very caution; I had my Sunday suit on. The edges of the fast water were very slippery. I walked on land through these areas; the bigger guys wanted to brag that they walked the ice for two miles, but not me. After about two miles we came to a large body of smooth water, perfect for skating. We were all running and sliding. I got a big running start and slid toward a frosty-looking area. When I hit this spot the ice crumbled, and down I went into about four feet of water. You don't do this alone. Luckily I was with older guys, and they came to my rescue. Getting back on the ice, I thought I was freezing. They carried me to the bank. Pete, my cousin, started a fire, and they undressed me and hung my clothes over the fire to dry. They gave me a warm jacket until my clothes dried. I sat by the warm fire. After my clothing dried we walked to the railroad track and headed for home. My clothing was a mess, no creases, just hanging loose; the suit was a fluffy mess. Man, I hated to go home like that. I just hoped Dad wasn't there. We separated and each of us went to his own home. Luckily for me, when I got home Dad was gone. Mom met me at the door. She said, "Where in the world have you been? You are a mess. Are you okay?" I was starving.

I changed clothes and ate dinner. Now I had supervision after church; no more paling around with the big guys.

Dad bought another cow, a small tan-colored jersey. The cow was in heat (wanting a boyfriend). Dad said, "You think you can be trusted to take the cow to Mr. Rivercombs?" He had a farmer about three miles up the road. It was closer walking the railroad track. Well, this could be exciting, and they were beginning to trust me. Old Nelly and I walked very nicely for about half the distance. I was getting a little tired, and I had an idea. If they can ride bulls, why can't I ride a cow? I had a little trouble mounting her; she wouldn't stand still. Finally I was on her, riding. I took it easy; I was sliding side to side, and when she ducked her head I would slip forward. I was riding high for about a mile until we came in hearing distance of that old bull. All at once old Nelly took off like a race horse, straight for the sound of that old bull. I held on for a second, but she was out of control—a runaway cow. She bounced me up, and I hit the ground feet first and running to keep from falling. Old Nelly seemed to know her way to the farm. Well, for once I wasn't hurt—no scars. I left her overnight at the farm. The next day we walked gently home; old Nelly had a smile on her face. She mooed a couple times as to say good-bye.

Wednesday is a church night; I had a difficult day once while writing these stories; however, I was going to class. Hurriedly I dressed. When reaching the parking lot I felt a little awkward walking into the classroom. When the class was over we stood around and talked for a while. The church is more like a family; the youngsters call you by your first name. Cory, a thirteen-year-old idled up to me and said, "Hank, you have on two different shoes." I looked down, and I couldn't believe what I saw, a dark shoe and a light tan shoe. I just said, "Oh, not again." This had happened before; it will be told in another story. In leaving I was stopped at the door. Danny and Audrey looked down and began to break up laughing. Embarrassed, I said, "And I have another pair just like them at home. Ha, ha."

Wayne was a friend of mine who had a paper route. I helped him on various occasions; my pay was a free movie. One day while we were waiting for the papers to come off the printing press, I cut initials in a tree. They were B S. While doing this the knife went closed, and I cut an eight-stitch gap in my finger. It was bandaged tightly. When Mom saw the bandage, she checked it out—nothing serious. She said, "What are we going to do with you? If you keep this up something serious is going to happen to you. Please be careful."

Another day I decided to stay inside the pressroom, hoping it would be safer. I was curious, with the dark, pudding-like ink. I checked it out for a while, and then I dipped up a finger full. I held my finger close to my eye and watched the ink flow gently down my finger. Suddenly, on purpose someone hit my elbow, and I had an eyeful of gooey black ink. Shutting my eyes tightly, I couldn't see anything. Someone from management came to the rescue. He wiped the contaminated area free of the ink; however, it penetrated the skin. I carried a black eye for a month. When I closed my eyes I didn't see the culprit; no one would squeal on him.

This was the end of this partnership.

Sonny, my friend, had an uncle who had a farm; he raised pigs, cattle, and sheep. We hitchhiked to his location. His aunt and uncle were very nice to us; she prepared a meal with venison and gravy with biscuits. The farm fascinated me, especially how they confined the pigs with a single wire fence. The pigs were fed twice a day; morning feeding was called slop, mainly table food scraps mixed with Purina hog chow. In the afternoon they were fed ears of corn; each meal was put in a v-shaped trough. The pigs were contained in the area by an electrically charged wire. Once they touched the wire they were grounded, causing a shock. After a couple of shocks they wised up, staying away from the wire. Well, studying this, I had another bright idea. I took ears of corn wrapped twice with wire, placed the corn in the feeding trough, and extended the wiring over the charged wire and dropped it, making a connection. Now the corn was hot (wired); as the pigs began to eat, they touched the wired corn. You never heard such squealing, stomping, and running; it was as if they had hit a hornet nest. They tried eating several times, with the same effect. The next morning we went down to slop the pigs for the morning feeding. They refused to eat; they stayed away from the trough. Before we left the uncle was telling his wife, "I don't know what's wrong with those dumb pigs. They won't eat." After we departed we heard that his uncle moved the feeding area away from the fence and made rectangular feeding troughs. The pigs were now on schedule eating again.

A lesson learned—you can train with a hot wire.

When getting back to nature, Glenn and I rented horses for a half day in the Dolly Ann area. This is where they mined iron ore; the terrain was rough. There were trails wide enough for a single vehicle, where along the stream big boulders were pushed out to the edge of the trail. Glenn was an excellent rider; he flew like the wind on horseback without a saddle and holding onto the mane. I was a novice, a more cautious rider; however, on this occasion I wanted to feel the excitement and the breeze of this fast-running horse.

As I was in high gear, flying down the trail, I saw a car in the close distance. Trees and bolders were on both sides; I didn't know what to do. At this speed I couldn't stop. A flash thought was to jump the car. No, no, I figured the horse knew more about this situation than me. I pulled the reins to the right, and the horse responded. I was letting the horse do its thing; it tried going by the car. It hit a large boulder and turned a flip; off I went like a belly dive, sliding about fifteen feet. All at once the horse's hindquarters landed beside me. The horse got to its feet before I did. Finally, scared to death, I wobbled to my feet. I checked myself for damages. I had on a white wool sweater with a class emblem on it; the sweater was stretched down to my ankles. I looked like someone dressed from the twenties. It would have fit a giraffe. I couldn't believe I wasn't hurt, so I rechecked myself again. The horse seemed stable; it let me mount, and I rode to the corral. Well, this was my last conflict with a horse. When Glenn returned, he was full of laughter. He said the next time try the pony or donkey. I wasn't happy with the teasing. All I said was, "This mishap stays here; keep it to yourself."

There was no reason for Mom and Dad to find this out. I would be grounded forever.

Christmas is a great time of the year. We didn't know what Dad and Mom had planned for us. We would ask for certain things, but the most exciting was the items we didn't know about. My main thing was hunting and fishing. I asked for fishing equipment; the girls wanted clothes and dolls, except for Dorothy, who wanted sports equipment. This was good; she shared them with me. Dreama wanted a record player; Lovera asked for makeup (she was already beautiful). Christmas morning when I woke up there was about eight inches of snow. Dad and the rest of the family were up. The girls seemed very happy as they opened their packages.

Christmas is a special time of the year; it is a time for giving, and Christ gave his life for us.

We never knew what Mom and Dad would give us. Although we let them know in advance what we wanted, they usually give us what we want. The excitement is receiving the things we didn't ask for. Dad was much like a kid himself; he couldn't wait until Christmas morning. He always wanted to give it earlier. My sisters, Lavera, Dorothy, and Dreama, were up before me; I came on the scene a little later. They seemed happy unwrapping their gifts; everyone had received what they asked for and even more. I unwrapped fishing equipment and was happy. Dad said, "What is this behind the tree?" Checking it out, it had my name on it. I thought, "Great, another fishing pole."

This was a surprise when I opened it. There was a gun; it was a 250-3000 Savage rifle, just like the one in the magazine Dad gave me to read. Now I know why he wanted me to read that article. I was real pleased, and then I began to think, Mom and Dad are good to us all year, and especially at Christmas. I had a guilty and sorrowful feeling. I hadn't given Dad anything, just problems throughout the year. Then I thought, "Jesus gave us his all; he didn't expect anything in return." I now know it's not the receiving but the giving that counts. After all the excitement, Dad asked, "How would you like to try out your gun?" "Great, this is a real gift." Before leaving Mom spoke up and said, "You all should stay home on Christmas Day." Mom was outvoted two to one. Her comment was, "Be careful and don't stay late; we will have dinner at four."

Up the mountain we drove until we came to the lead ridge to the top. We began walking; the snow was deep and slippery. As we reached the summit the snow was deeper. We came across a fresh bear track. Dad decided to track it, hoping it would go into a den or a hollow tree. Well, this didn't happen. This was a smart bear. He knew where to scrape for water and acorns. We followed him about two hours; that's equal to three miles. The bear began biting off small branches. Dad said, "He is getting ready to bed down." We walked about twenty-five feet on each side of the tracks, hoping the bear might be bedded down and would jump out where we could get a shot. I began to lag behind. Dad came over and said, "Are you getting tired?" I said, "A little." Dad stopped and scraped the snow back. He gathered dry branches and built a fire. He made sure the fire was burning good; he laid extra pieces of wood to add to the fire. He said, "Stay here and keep warm. I will try to catch up to him." While he was gone it seemed forever. Dad returned a short time later; he said the bear was on the point of a ridge, and it could see in all directions. "When I approached, it jumped before I could get a shot," he said. We started for home; the snowdrifts were very high. We saw a deer in a drift up to its stomach. Season wasn't in for deer, and I was glad. Dad was getting tired. To encourage him, I said, We will be on the down grade, and it will be much easier walking without drifts." I said, "When we get home Mom will have a nice Christmas dinner ready." We were both encouraged by this conversation. How happy we were to be home in a warm place by the fire.

CHAPTER III

High School Era

W HEN WE WERE growing up, firecrackers were part of our recreation until they were illegal. I have enjoyed the excitement of fireworks. I experimented with soda and vinegar, just got a fizzing effect. Also, carbide would make an explosion when placed in a sealed container, with drops of water added; also, it would make a flame from the gasses when lit with a match. Coal miners would use carbide in lamps that put off a gas flame for light. All this was messy and was limited in where I could use it. Striking matches fascinated me; with a little friction, you get an explosive flame. This gave me an idea. I could remove about ten match heads and compress them in a one-inch nut with bolts screwed in from both sides, causing it to be friction tight. When throwing this handmade grenade against a hard surface, it would explode. I explained this theory to my Jeter School classmates; they wanted to see if it would work. During recess, I had all the necessary parts. I placed each component in its proper place. I screwed the bolts in on both sides of the nut, sandwiching them until getting a snug fit. Behind me at about forty yards was a three-story building. I threw the handmade grenade against the old cement high school. It went off, vibrating the ground. The bolts and nut separated, and a bolt went through the upstairs window, breaking the glass. It worked. I got a little cheering from the onlookers. I went back to class as if nothing had happened. About an hour later the homeowner contacted the school principal and made a complaint; he brought the bolt as evidence. The school speakers came on, and the students were asked if anyone had any knowledge of this event. All I can say is, thanks for a group of tight-lipped buddies. I was safe. Don't try this. Someone could be seriously hurt, especially you or me.

Jeter was a fun school; I enjoyed shop, physical education, gym, and other classes. There were a lot of girls; Betty stood out among them all. She sat in the desk behind me. I spent 75 percent of my time facing backward. The teacher would say, "Mr. Forbes, face the front."

One-day in gym a group was playing basketball. There were players of various ages and sizes. I thought this looked to be a safe and interesting game. They were throwing the ball up and down the court to one another and shooting for the basket, so I decided to participate. They put me in a position; I was a novice, not familiar with the game. They passed the ball to me; I shot and missed the basket. I was not that good, and I think they wanted a replacement. As the game progressed I turned to locate the ball, and, to my surprise, in front of my face was the ball. It looked twice its size as it bounced off my head. I woke up. Someone with a wet napkin was rubbing my face, and some bystanders were looking down, I staggered off the court, never to challenge that sport. I learned to avoid dangerous sports. Mom would not even let me play football. She said, "Play in the band with your dad's double bass horn."

Another day I decided to play alone to avoid contact sports. There was an eight-foot monkey bar near a ten-foot fence. I climbed upon the fence about four feet and jumped for the bar. I got a good swing back and forth. I did this several times; it was a lot of fun. I decided if four feet was this much fun I would climb higher and get a better swing. I tried jumping several times from the upper location, and I was getting a better swing. Trying for a gold ribbon, I got on top of the fence. I was a little wiggly at this height. I made a great jump; when hitting the bar my hands slipped. I turned a perfect flip, only landing on my head. When I woke up everyone was saying that was a great jump (poor landing). The kids helped me up. I was late returning to my classes. At home Mom would say, "Where did you get those bruises?"

Dad helped me get a motor bike. It was a Roadmaster bike with a Wizard engine. Mr. Henderson helped me to put it together. It ran like a charm and cost only pennies a day. I did not need a permit to operate it. It was good transportation and great fun to ride. I rode my bike to school at Rivermont Graded School and back home for lunch. There was a neighbor who lived next to the main highway; he had a sassy dog that did not like the motor sound. The moment I got within sound distance that dog was waiting on me; he thought he owned the highway. He would come at me head first, barking and growling. For a small dog, he was not afraid of anything. To keep from hitting him he would force me out of the road; when passing him he would bite at my feet, which were on the pedals. I slowed down, and his momentum carried him in front again. I opened the throttle to a higher speed, when I cut to miss him, he also cut the same direction; we had a head-on collision.

The bike and I turned a flip; when it landed, it broke off one of the pedals.

The dog took off running and yelping. I knew at that speed he was not hurt; luckily, I wasn't hurt. I picked up my bike, pushed it home, and parked it. My next move was getting my Remington 16-gauge shotgun loaded with buckshot. I had the intent of dog hunting, and blowing that pest away. Dad caught me going out the door with the gun. He said, "You are not going hunting! This is a school day." I said, "I'm not going hunting; I am going to kill that Barnet dog that has been pestering me and caused me to wreck on my bike." Dad caught me by the shoulder; with the other hand he retrieved the shotgun. He said, "This is a talking solution, not a dog war." Well, after a positive talk, I walked to school late. Now I had to explain my tardiness. In trouble again, with study hall. Seemed I couldn't win for losing.

To keep out of trouble I decided to sell the bike. I sold it to a friend (Johnny, the one I put to sleep) who worked at White Sulphur, West Virginia, twenty miles away. I sold him the bike for $195 with a deposit of $15 down and a promise to pay the balance in monthly payments. That was a big mistake; he did not keep his promise. Dad took me to where he was boarding in West Virginia; I ask if John was rooming there. The proprietor said he no longer lived there; he did not pay his rent, and he was put out. I asked if he had a motor bike. He replied, "Yes. I am holding it for payment." I explained that it was my bike. He said, "And it is your loss." I left and returned with a West Virginia state officer. I showed him the ownership papers from Virginia and said, "You have in your possession a stolen bike that has been transferred across state lines." The officer explained the circumstances and said, "Do you know the penalty of this theft, having stolen property from across state lines?" At last I was on the winning side. The culprit gave up the bike and offered to pay for any inconveniences. Dad was happy. He just said, "Remember my come easy statement." We loaded up the bike and headed home. I thanked the officer.

While writing these stories, I developed a voice change. I went to a specialist; after a brief examination and reviewing my x-rays he determined I had a sinus problem that was causing voice change and vertigo. It caused dizziness (in a joking manner someone said, "I have always been dizzy"); the doctor gave me antibiotics and suggested I get therapy. Well, I had never had therapy on my head. On the first session (at home), the therapist explained a theory. He suggested that we try moving my head in various positions. This went on for about fifteen minutes. I could see no improvement'; I was dizzy. We came back into another room and replaced my glasses, and he explained a timetable for additional therapy. He left, and I went back to what I was doing prior to his visit. I was reading the Bible daily in order to complete it in one year. I noticed I was having a problem seeing the fine print; I cleaned the glasses, but there was no improvement. Later I was back at writing; I had a problem seeing what I was writing. I thought my eyes were tired, or it was some effect from the therapy. I also had a similar problem watching television. The next day I began reading again, and the problem was still there. My glasses were only a month old, so it could not be them. I examined the glasses, adjusting them in various positions without any improvement. I removed the glasses and closely examined them. These glasses had a frame all around the lens. My glasses only had the frame around the top portion. Dum dee dum. I had on the wrong glasses; I recovered my glasses in the therapy area. I put them on, and my sight problem was solved (another senior moment).

While in high school, Dad bought me a service cycle. It was manufactured by Simplex Corporation. It was a beautiful machine, with wind shield and whitewall tires. The fenders and wheels were chrome; it had crash bars and leather saddlebags with tassels. Man, I felt like the king of the road. It also had a double-spring seat; now I could double with Betty, my favorite buddy (girlfriend to be). After getting a little good on handling the bike I would go into a filling station for gasoline. I would lean it over on its side, open it up, and spin around the gas pumps, similar to riding in a drum. I was really hot dogging it. Riding on the road, I had a green light. I speeded up and leaned the bike to the left; the crash bars hit the asphalt, and I slid under a parked wood truck. Boy, was I lucky. I was okay; however, my butt itched a little, as to have a strawberry on it. I rode down to the filling station. While in the bathroom I examined my butt. I had the teeth of a comb stuck in my rear. Well, it hurt a lot more coming out than going in. In the future I rode less dangerously, knowing what gravity can cause. I couldn't expose Betty to such dangers. At home, Mom asked, "Why are you limping?" I did not want the cycle locked up, so I said nothing.

I skipped school one afternoon and decided to go hunting. I got my gun, hopped on the cycle, and up the mountain I went. I parked the cycle and quietly walked to a favorite location and sat down. Woodcutters had taken trees from this area, and two of their horses were feeding on acorns. I was a little disgusted, thinking the horses would scare off any game. I was about to move when I heard a put-put, then a calk. Turkeys were feeding on the opposite direction of the horses. I lifted the automatic shotgun, took aim, and fired. The lead turkey fell; another one flew up, lighting on a tree limb. I aimed and blasted it. Well, I never heard such commotion; those two horses looked like a Wild West show. They were kicking, whinnying and bucking. You would have thought bees were attacking them. When things quieted down I went over, picked up the two turkeys, got on the cycle, and headed home. Down the mountain I went. The faster I went, the more those birds flopped their wings out, as if they were taking off. They were about to cause me to lose control. I slowed to a stop, tied the wings, and took off again. As I continued home, I rode slowly by O. E. Parker Company, hoping they would see my trophies. They recognized me and said, "Hankie, turkey season is not in; you better get home quick before a game warden sees you." Mom was happy to get the turkeys. Dad was not in too good of a mood. He said, "You will never learn. If you keep this up, I am going to put a lock on your ride. And besides that, aren't you supposed to be in school?"

It was time for a change; two boys together means trouble. I did not like doing things alone. I was also tired of my school buddies, and they reminded me of my past problems.

Betty and I were in the same classes, and we spent quality time together. She was a Christian and often talked church to me, especially if I got off on the wrong subject. She helped me from getting in a lot of trouble. We often doubled on my service cycle; I had it under control—no more foolishness. Betty could handle herself on the ride; she had good balance. She was excellent at knowing which way to lean as we challenged curves and turns.

I asked Dad and Mom if I could ride to Aunt Nell's, which is about forty miles. They agreed. I asked Betty if she would like to take a ride over North Mountain to Aunt Nell's. She said yes, if it was okay with my mother it was okay with her mother. She did not say anything to her dad; he was a little resentful toward me. We dressed properly, and off we went. It was a nice day and a lot of fun riding the mountain curves. The cycle rode well, and we did not encounter any problems. There was a little traffic but not heavy. It was more fun going down the mountain than going up. Betty was a true sport; she trusted me not to let her get hurt. We cautiously turned into a dirt road leading to the farm on White Rock Mountain. When we arrived they were glad to see us. Uncle George had just returned from the fields. They both loved Betty and were glad to see her again. I helped Uncle George with his chores; Betty was in the kitchen with Aunt Nell. I think they had the first great room. It was a kitchen and rec room with tv and a daybed, plus dining table and chairs, and it was heated with the wood cookstove. They raised cattle, chickens, and other animals besides farming. They raised corn, wheat, hay, and a crop of berries. On the side porch a tame chicken laid her eggs in a nest. As I checked it out a big blacksnake was in the nest curled up and had swallowed four unbroken eggs; they were within the snake, looking like lumps.

Uncle George caught it by the tail and lifted it out; they do not kill the blacksnakes because they feed on mice.

There was a springhouse with water from the mountain running through it. Here they kept milk from the cattle, and other perishable things. I helped my uncle separate cream from milk; he would take the cream to the market and make buttermilk from the balance. They also made their own butter in a wooden churn. While Betty was helping Aunt Nell, we packed berries from the springhouse, placing them in baskets to sell at the market. The market was in Lexington, eight miles away. He made a sign saying, "berries 12 cents a basket." We weren't doing too good on sales. Uncle George said, "We have to advertise better, and make people think they are getting a bargain. He made a new sign: "berries two baskets for 25 cents." To my surprise, he sold all the berries (he was a fox). We went back to the farm. Aunt Nell had supper ready. It included fried chicken, smothered-in-butter cream gravy mashed potatoes, and berries floating in cream. Now I knew why she was heavy; she was a wonderful cook, using a lot of farm-fresh butter and cream.

Betty helped her clean the kitchen; we said thanks for everything and headed home. When at home, Betty's dad told her, "I saw Hank going up North Mountain with a girl on the back of that put-put; she was holding tight around his waist. Betty just smiled, and her mother said nothing.

When I was in high school I was in D.O. diversified occupation class; we went to class for two-thirds of the day and worked a job one-third of the school day. We were graded according to our on-the-job potential. One of my jobs was at a filling station. We washed, waxed, changed oil, greased, and changed tires. I was working for Craighead and Farley, who also participated in the job functions. This was a fun job. You met a lot of people. It also gave me spending money. G. C. would pitch in and help me wash cars on Saturday. He was always joking, and it didn't even seem like work. Together we could wash one-hundred-plus cars on a full Saturday. We also washed a panel bread truck. To make it easier to wash, they bought a handle type brush, I could reach the higher locations without a ladder. It worked really well on the truck.

Charlie brought his shiny new Chevy in to be washed (it really did not need it). He was very particular, not even finger prints. I took my shoes off when washing the interior. I decided to use the brush on Charlie's car; it might save a little time. Well, I washed his car. When wiping the car down with a squeegee, it looked like a million tiny scratches. It had so much wax on it that the brush cut small groves in it. I went to G. C. and said, "I have ruined Charlie's wax job." G. C. had a saying, 80-0e-80, that meant "big stuff." When he saw the car he said, "Charlie is going to kill us; he is picking the car up in thirty minutes. We have no time to lose. Get the wax and polish cloth. We both took a side. G. C. was huffing and puffing. He finished his side and started the hood on my side. The car was finished. G. C. looked it over and said, "Hank, you owe me. I pulled you out of this one. This is the fastest wax job we have ever done." At that moment Charlie came in, looked at his Chevy and said, "Ain't that a beauty? Looks like it's just been waxed. Both G. C. and I grinned and agreed. G. C. saved the day.

Charlie's car was a jinx. Charlie's next trip to the station was for an oil change. G. C. was the co captain in this area; he was very busy, but was interrupted often when changing Charlie's oil. The job was finished, and G. C. removed the car from the bay (lift). Charlie paid for the oil change and took off for the ten-mile trip home. After driving five miles, that car started sputtering. The radiator boiled over, and the car died, and would not even turn over. After a quick examination they found no—yes, no—oil in the engine. This is a big 80 0e 80. G. C. forgot to put oil in Charlie's car (too many interruptions). Charlie was furious. I was glad I wasn't the culprit. Maybe my luck was rubbing off on G. C. The insurance company gave Charlie a new engine. He was happy with this and remained a good customer.

On another occasion, a high roller friend of Craighead brought in his fastback Cadillac for service. After the service was completed, the car was parked in the wash bay. It was the filthiest car I have ever seen; it would be a beauty if washed and waxed. Although they did not ask for either, I decided to wash and wax it. The more I rubbed the duller it got. Not even compound would cut the crud. Finally, I decided to use a solution that we used to clean whitewall tires. I tried washing the hood with it, leaving it on about two minutes and rinsing it off. The hood looked great. I tried each side of the top and got the same results. I thought, "This is working good, and with less rubbing." Finally, I started on the side panels. It ran down the sides, creating streaks with shiny areas. I cleaned it up the best I could and washed the tires and wheels. Well, it did not look like it did when they brought it in; however, it was clean. I only hope I did not ruin a paint job. All were happy. When leaving they gave me a $10 tip for parking the car in a clean area; they did not notice the streaks.

Another one of my jobs was with Southern Bakery. They processed bread from start to finish. They mixed flour components into dough, placed it into loaf pans, and baked it in a large oven. It was placed on racks to cool. After cooling, it was transferred to the bread slicing machine, sliced and wrapped, then loaded on delivery trucks. I worked on the slicing and wrapping machine. This production job kept you busy. You placed loaves in the track area and gave it a push, and the lugs carried the loaf through the slicer (a group of many blades). After being sliced, it was lifted to the next level, where it was wrapped. It was a dangerous job. The slicing blades were positioned according to slice thickness; they were in a frame that had a continuous up and down motion. As the loaf passed through, it was sliced. This was an area where the bread could jam and stop the machine. On one occasion I shut the machine down; it had an off/on button. I put my hand in to retrieve the bread. I jogged the machine, hitting and releasing the start button. The loaf behind hit my hand, pushing it up into the lift position. My hand and fingers were caught and pinched in this lift position. My hand was not stuck tight; I removed it slowly so as not to hit the blades. The skin on my hand was torn from the end of my finger to my wrist. I shut the machine down, wrapped a clean towel around the area, and went to the first aid area. When they cleansed the skin from my hand and bandaged it, I began to shake. Also, I was sick on my stomach.

I just realized I could have lost my hand. I was excused from work. I hated to go home and explain this to my parents. Mom checked me out, and seeing only a scar, she said, "Young man, this is the end of you working." I was glad for her decision. Now I had more time for other activities and to spend with Betty.

The Greenbrier Hotel was owned by the C & O Railroad. It was being completely renovated. John P. Pettyjohn and Adams co. was the contractor. I got a ride to the location with John, who worked there. I was on summer vacation. After talking to personnel for a short review of my qualifications, he explained, "You are only fourteen; we do not hire anyone under sixteen." I explained how responsible I was and that my work ethics were as an eighteen-year-old. He finally said, "I will hire you on a temporary basis. If you mess up and don't take orders, you are gone." I had nothing to worry about; I have always been a good worker. I even do more than expected. I just have a problem with accidents. I worked hard and tried to prove myself. As jobs were finished I would go to another position. I got a lot of experience in positions from labor to jack hammer, painting and errand boy. The Friday workday was ending, and we started home. I asked John if he would let me out at Mr. Sheppard's store. All the guys were chewing Beechnut tobacco. It looked like they enjoyed it. I went in and purchased a bag. On the walk home, about a quarter of a mile, I began to chew. The juice was burning my throat. I thought I would get over it. I reached home a little pale. Mom said, "Are you sick?" "No," I replied while juice was dripping down my lips. She saw what I was chewing and chased me out the back door. I must have swallowed some juice. I vomited, and she got a cold, wet cloth and placed it on my head. Chewing is not a good idea. Those workers were faking it. Another lesson learned: do not do bad habits.

Dad was going fishing on the Shenandoah River. He did not invite me.

I had previously caught our favorite fish bait, lizards, crayfish and madtoms; they are a small breed of catfish,. I offered them to Dad for his trip. I guess he felt a little guilty, and he asked if I would like to go with him. Well he fell into my trap; the bait was for this intent. We left with Mom's approval; she said, "Do not let anything happen to Hankie." Dad puffed a little and said, "What do you think I am?" Therefore, off we went. Mr. Sedrick had a farm with the south fork of the river running through the property. He also had guest cabins to accommodate fishermen. Off we went; we reached the farm about four in the afternoon. The main house was positioned high on a hill overlooking the river and the guest cabins; it was a place of beauty. Mr. Sedrick met us with a friendly welcome. He said the fishing is good. "After you get settled in the madam has a layout of food prepared; follow me to the house," he said. We sat down at a huge table; it consisted of southern fried chicken, mashed potatoes, beans, salads, and some delicious-looking pies. I can't remember saying grace, although I knew we should be thankful for the safe trip and this food. We ate and enjoyed everything, including the conversation and the fellowship. As we were leaving he said breakfast was at six o'clock. We thanked the madam and went to the cabin for the night. I slept off and on, thinking about the next day's fishing. We got up early, cleaned up, and headed for the farmhouse. Everything was prepared. I was not too hungry because of the amount I ate the night before. I didn't want that food to be wasted, so I ate moderately. After breakfast, we thanked them both and left for the river. The river was beautiful, with crystal clear water and some ledges and deep troughs. We entered the water on the shallows and fished as we waded. The ledges were about two feet deep and the drop-off to about six feet; it was perfect for fish to hide. We would cast into the ledges, and our bait would drift into the deeper holes of water. You fished this area very cautiously. Standing near one of the ledges I hooked a nice one, and in the excitement I stepped off the ledge. I held on to the pole; all you could see was the top of my head. Having a little difficulty, Dad came over and pulled me to the shallows. I held on to the pole and the sixteen-inch bass. Dad spoke a little positive; he said to be more careful. Dad caught several nice bass, one was eighteen inches. He also caught a huge channel catfish about two feet long. It had dark speckles on the white surface of the skin (catfish do not have scales). I was happy for Dad. While fishing I did not notice the line tangling around the reel gears and bail. I stayed in the water to repair the problem—big mistake. I looked up, and Dad was motioning for me to go to the bank for repairs. I ignored him, and he began pointing down in the water. Well, he was right. I dropped the drag nut, it went into an area, and I couldn't retrieve it. I sat on the bank the rest of the day. It was awesome watching a pro at his best. Luckily, I brought another reel with me.

Dad's brother and Mr. Gibson came the next day. We went to a location where we used boats. I was with Mr. Gibson. As we were fishing, he broke off from a hang-up and he began stringing out line. He said, "Hankie, hand me a hook and a madtom." I gave him the leader hook and a golden tom. He hooked it through the lips, and he started to drop it into the water. I said no, no, he did not have it tied to his line (this was something I might do). I was broke up trying not to laugh. I watched the tom swim off. Nodding his head, he said he would have to have a drink on that one. I think that might have been the problem. Dad and I laughed about this on the way home. Mr. Gibson and Dad's brother stayed for another day of fishing. I would have liked to stay and observe this.

CHAPTER IV

Covington Era

D AD BEGAN TO trust me. He decided to let me drive the station wagon on certain occasions. I guess he thought it safer than the service cycle. Since I didn't work evenings, Betty and I had more time together, I thought this was getting serious. A cousin of hers wanted to go to Buena Vista, about sixty miles, to visit a friend. We decided to drive her there; we did not have our parents' consent. Reaching our destination, we parked in a manufacturing parking lot, unaware of a two-foot pipe sticking out of the ground. It was about fender high. We were there for about twenty minutes and decided to go to another location. Not knowing about the post, I made a sharp turn, and suddenly there was a thump, and the car stopped. Oh no, I thought, this could not be. I jumped out to see the problem, and, sure enough, the fender was caved in. I cautiously backed away so as not to do additional damage. We drove back to Covington. I did not dare to let Dad see the car in that condition. We let Betty's mother know of our fate. I called home and asked if I could spend the night with a friend. Mom said, "Okay, but you be good and don't get hurt (stay out of trouble). We knew Slick and Viola (a nice black family), who owned a repair shop. We drove to the location. While I was talking to Slick, Betty went in and talked to Viola. He said, "Drive the car into the shop. Let's take a look and see the damages (it was 11:00 p.m.). I first asked how long it would take, then how much it would cost. He explained, "It is not cheap; I need to do body work, prime, sand, and paint and allow drying time before buffing. It will take about seven hours." I asked about the price. I said, "I do not have much money." He said, "Give me $20.00 and you can pay me a little each week." Wow, that was a load off my mind. He completed the job before 5:00 a.m. I was happy and said thanks to them. I cleaned up and changed clothes and went to school. After school, I returned the car home as if nothing had happened. That little venture made a dent in my spending money. If I had asked Dad, he would have said no to this adventure. Well, another lesson learned.

In school, I was not too good in English. I was the worst speller, and I spelled as it sounds. Also, I didn't like being confined to reading (literature). Betty noticed I was behind on book reports; she volunteered to help me out. She was an excellent reader and liked to read; she read the books I was behind in and wrote the reports. I think these were the first As I ever made. She also cleaned and manicured my dirty fingernails. She corrects my spelling to this day. I began spending more time with her in and out of school. I began to miss Betty when she was not around. We would even go fishing and hunting together; she was a real sport (buddy).

We were on a date. As we drove down the street, someone threw an object and hit the station wagon. I did not know if it was an apple, rock, or baseball. Furious, I decided to back up to the area that it was thrown from—another bad decision. I backed into a telephone pole, scraping the back fender. To this day, I am not at my best when backing up. The culprit was nowhere in sight. I examined the fender; it had a slight ding in it, and also streaks of creosote from the pole. Betty was getting a little braver. She said, "Your dad is going to take your driving privileges. You are too reckless; you should think before you act." I could not be mad; she hit the nail on the head. This was good advice. I decided to go by the station where I worked and try some repairs. The bay was open, and I drove in and washed the fender to examine the damages. I used a rubber hammer, hitting behind the ding, and it popped out, no damage to the paint. I used rubbing compound in the area of the creosote streaks. They were gone when I washed the fender, and luck was with me. Now I had a car with one clean fender. To avoid washing the whole car, I sprinkled dust from a garden compound on it. Now I had a dirty car and fender. Well, another lesson learned: don't back up; pull up.

In graded school there was a bully named Buddy; he was imposing in every game he played. On two occasions he made me fighting mad; however, I contained myself, since he was larger than me. On occasion we were pitching pennies to see who was closest to the line. Buddy would pick up the coins and put them in his pocket, not to return them. On another occasion I was flipping coins; he would reach out and catch them, refusing to give them back. I avoided a fight, but I did not forget his actions. He was a grade ahead of me, so I avoided him as much as possible. This was at Rivermont School. We were transferred to Jeter, and I did not encounter him there. Finally, our next class was at Covington High. In high school, we were in the same physical ed class. We were playing touch football (you would block or just touch to stop a forward movement). Here again, macho Buddy had to prove his authority. He was playing too rough for touch ball; he was dressed in a band uniform for the evening game. I did not start fights or problems; however, I was known to end them. As we proceeded with the touch game, Buddy blocked me, sticking out his leg and jerking me over it to the ground. I got up with my shirt half torn off. I just gave him a look and started walking off the field. There was an audience, that side of the building's windows were full of bystanders. Buddy hollowed out (so everyone could hear him), "Forbes, you aren't scared, are you?" I stopped, turned around, and said, "I am not walking so fast that you can't catch up to me (now was the time to get even). Trying to showboat, he came rushing toward me while I was standing firmly. With both fists he hit me in the stomach. I went back at about a fifteen-degree angle, clinched my fist, and, using the weight I had, I went forward, striking him right above the right eye (he didn't know what hit him). Down he went in that nice band uniform. To attack his masculinity, I pounced down on him like fleas on Fido. I imagined his face as a punching bag. I worked it over; there was not a spot I did not hit. His face black and blue, eyes swelled shut, lips swelled and bleeding, I finally got off him. There was a lot of cheering from the school windows, but he was in no condition to hear it. I walked to the school door; there was no available stretcher, so a couple of his friends got him to his feet, placed his arms over their shoulders, and dragged him into the building with his feet dragging. They took him into the infirmary. I went to class. Later one of his friends came in and ask if they could be excused to take him to the doctor; they thought his eye was dislocated. Well, I didn't have any problems with him for the rest of our acquaintance; he carried a lump (goose egg) above his right eye as a constant reminder of his unfortunate behavior. We worked in the same location after high school. He became my best friend. All was forgiven and forgotten, and we lived in the same neighborhood.

I was seventeen when I graduated from high school. Betty, still in school, was fifteen. She was one-half grade ahead; however, she lacked a couple credits to finish. I was still working at Craighead & Farley; they increased my pay, and I was saving a little money between dates. We spent a lot of time together; however, she was still in school, and I thought someone else might show interest in her, so I decided (at eighteen) to ask if she would marry me. This was a big decision; with my little job, it would take a lot of courage. With no vehicle and no starting money for rent, lights, insurance, and water and sewer, this seemed impossible. Betty's answer was, "I want to finish school first; with me working we would have a better future." She was right, but I was selfish and looking out for what I wanted. After some persuasion, I talked her into asking her mother if she would approve. I knew my parents would not. To my surprise, Mrs. Southers knew how I felt about Betty; she approved and asked if we needed finances for our adventure. We decided to go to North Carolina (run away) and get married at Reidsville. Mrs. Southers gave Betty a sum of money, and off we went.

We stopped at the C & O hospital in Clifton Forge and got the results of our blood test. I called Mom and asked if it was okay for me to go out of town with a friend (there was an out-of-town football game).

We arrived in Reidsville about 3:00 p.m. There was a justice of the peace, where a marriage license could be obtained. We lied about our age, sixteen and eighteen. The first thing I knew, we were in front of the justice of the peace with two witnesses taking our marriage vows. It did not seem like we were getting married because of the joke telling by the witnesses during the ceremony. After the marriage was completed, we went to a motel to freshen up; later we went out for dinner. We were very excited and happy on our way home. I was uneasy as to what my parents would say. Betty told her Dad. I told my mom of the marriage; she cried a little and was not too happy with me. She thought we were too young. We did not have an apartment; Mom said, "You and Betty can use your bedroom until something better is worked out." This worked out, we made a two-room apartment at Betty's home. Dad bought us a refrigerator; we bought the rest of our needs from Mrs. Sneed, who ran a furniture store and sold on time. One day as I was walking to the station to work, Mr. Mcallister picked me up. He was a local (Christian) contractor. He said, "Hampie, where are you going this early?" I replied, "To work." He said, "How much do you earn on that job?" I explained, and he said, "How would you like to work for me and make $10 more a week (that was a big raise for those times). Well, I went with him to work that morning. Craighead and Farley were scratching their heads when I walked in that afternoon and told them I accepted another job. They just said that if it didn't work out to come back and see them. I just hoped that G. C. and Claude would understand.

This was a good change. I could get experience in preparing and leveling foundations, mixing mud and laying cinderblocks, and also framing. The only part that needed improvement was digging foundations and footers. Mr. Mcallister believed in doing this by hand instead of using equipment. (I think this was his future downfall, not growing with the times.) When supplies were needed, I picked them up in his old International truck at O. E. Parker's Lumber Co. Amazingly, I was working without any accidents; I thought I must be growing up. I did not have a watch; I drove a large peg in the ground at the end of the shadow (caused by the shade from the sun). I placed a smaller peg, at the end of each hour. I placed another peg until I had twelve, pegs, one for each hour of the day. Now I had a sundial for telling time.

We were expecting our first child, and we needed to save money. We moved back to Mom and Dad's house.

When picking up supplies for Mr. Mc. I was familiar with the OEP merchandise layout. I often picked out supplies and loaded the order for them. This saved me time. One day when I was checking out the load, Carl (the co-owner) said, "Hankie why don't you consider working for us? We can start you at $85 every two weeks; you can go out on the construction sites, and the pay will be increased." I told him I would think about it. The offer was $5 more a week; this doesn't sound like much; however, it was an advancement to accomplish more.

I went to Mr. Mc. and told him about the offer. He said business was getting a little slow, and it would be months before he could give me an increase. He advised me to take the offer. He also said, "I hate to lose you, but if you have any trouble on the job come back and see me." I took the job with Carl at O. E. Parker's. I could save money while living at home; we would need it when the baby came. Betty was seeing Dr. Johnson, our family (black) doctor.

We didn't have money enough to cover a hospital bill. Dr Johnson, with his nurse (also African American), delivered the baby at home. He was smart enough to know Betty might have problems delivering because of a deformed pelvis. He brought oxygen tanks with him, which were needed. He delivered us a four pound six ounce boy; he was not a full nine-month baby. Doc revived him, and he was rushed to the C & O hospital, where he was put in an incubator. The family called me from work, and I was there in time go with him to the hospital. His name is Hampton Edward Forbes III. He recovered after two weeks and has been a live wire ever since. He has a fair complexion and red hair, like my mother; this made him something special. My dad was like a proud peacock. I have some stories to tell about him at the proper time.

While at work, I was ripping a four-foot board. It requires two people to handle this; however, I was in a hurry, and no one was around. I tried it alone.

As it got close to the end of the cut, the saw pinched, caught half of the board, and shot it over my head; splinters were flying. I looked around, and no one was watching. I was lucky. I learned that you do not do a two-man job with one person.

Needing a job with benefits and more pay, I put in an application at Westvaco.

I explained to Carl that I could not put Betty at risk because of the lack of money, and I now had a family started that would require more income. Carl shook his head and said, "Hankie, we are a small company I can only give you an additional five-cent increase and put you to making cabinets and train you in the framing construction, where there is more money. Well, if he had offered me a dollar more I would not have taken it. Westvaco promotes according to your potential and position attitude. They called me for a labor position on the work pool. This is where they draw laborers from, placing them in other needed areas. I worked daily in various parts of the mill. I also worked all the overtime offered. As the first full-time job, I was transferred from the labor pool to the lime kiln area; this was a part of the chalk plant, where chalk was made from lime. This job required charging the kiln every hour with a ton of limestone rocks (loaded in a cart), three hundred pounds of coke (used to cook the rock), all loaded by hand. This was called the charge. The discharge was pulling thirteen hundred pounds of lime from the bottom of the kiln; this lime was taken to the second-floor level and put in a slacking tank. All this was a one-hour task. I was making $1.17 an hour. I liked overtime; it was double time. I often worked by kiln, and when there was a no-show for other kilns I would work them every other hour; they would pay me for twelve hours during an eight-hour shift (a lot of hustling). I often worked overtime as much as sixteen, twenty-four, thirty-two, and forty hours.

This area was physical labor—no mechanical help, just get 'er done.

Eight hour shift, you could take a nap or shower up, or you could load rocks for the next shift.

When preparing to work overtime, I would load up extra cars (these were like mining cars, which ran on rail tracks). I placed these cars on a sidetrack during an eight-hour shift; I had four on the sidetrack to be used on the next, overtime, shift. By doing this, I was more refreshed on the first shift and did not have to work so hard on the second shift. Three kilns were involved, each having a worker to maintain the charges. I worked with Harry and Brown, both of color; we got along well until someone began taking the cars from the sidetrack, which I had loaded. I questioned the loss; however, no one admitted being guilty. To solve this problem, I sprayed a small white dot on the backside of the cart wheel. Before the shift was over, another cart was missing. I watched for the return of the carts Harry brought down—the marked cart. I didn't confront him; I had another method in mind of bringing this to his attention.

We loaded coke from a large pile; to get to it there was a rail track with just enough width to get through to the coke pile. There was a boardwalk about forty feet above the cart track. When Harry went in to load coke, I went to the platform above, where I had previously put a forty-pound rock. I looked over the side and dropped a small pebble, noticing where it would hit. Finally, I found the exact place where his foot would be on the way out.

When he pushed his cart out, I waited until his foot hit my zero spot. I dropped the boulder; it hit behind his foot with a loud crash, splintering into minute pieces; it even splintered the tie. Harry looked up as if the sky was falling, with a whitish tint and eyes as big as tennis balls. Seeing me, he tried to speak, saying, "w . . . wh . . . wh . . . wh . . . what the—are you trying to do, kill me?" I replied, "The next car of rocks you steal, I am going to hit your head." Well, this broke him from his theft actions. The word got around. No more rocks were taken.

After working this area for a while, they gave me a promotion. This was a much easier job. They would truck in loads of lime and dump it near the tracks. I was required to load up cars of lime and take it to the second-floor slacking tank. (The slacked lime was used for making chalk.) I could do three or four loads an hour. This was an all-daylight job and just five days a week. (I wasn't getting any overtime.) During the summer your perspiration would mix with the lime dust and irritate your skin, sometime causing burns. I wore a scarf around my neck and a mask.

Every job has a smart rear end; it happened to be the oiler. This day he put heavy grease on my shovel handle. While in a hurry, I picked up the shovel, and, much to my surprise, I was loaded with grease—arms, legs, and side. He did not hide his actions. He was proud. He was standing around laughing, saying, "I got old Forbes." Some of the onlookers said he was in trouble: "You do not fool with Forbes." As time went by I obtained a pair of rubber gloves. I filled them with caustic and the same heavy grease. He was bragging of what he had pulled. I went up to him saying, You really got me," at the same time slapping him on the back and sliding the glove down his coveralls. It looked like a chocolate pie. I repeated the back slapping and bragging with him on his dirty work. Those standing around saw the payback. Well, within an hour, his shirt was full of holes and his coveralls were falling off. Seeing what I did to him, he was like a bantam rooster but doing nothing but grumbling. He didn't hang around my work area after that.

Carl, my boss at OEP, asked if I would like to go fishing at Gathright's. I was delighted to go; this was an area of the upper Jackson River, clean, pure, virgin water. It was a prime location. Only guests were allowed there. Mr. Gathrite had a somewhat rustic inn, which accommodated guests for hunting, fishing, and just a week's retreat. Carl and I drove to the location in Bath County. We pulled up to the location to let Mr. Gathrite know our fishing location. Carl gave Mr. Gathrite scrap lumber and other materials. In return, Mr. Gathrite gave Carl permission to fish.

Much to my surprise, Arthur Godfrey came out with a towel over his island print shirt and shorts. He was jogging to the river about a mile away for a swim. After getting permission, we headed for Carl's favorite spot (honey hole).

We entered the river in a rowboat. The river had a riverjacks bottom with small and larger rocks and ledges, perfect habitat for fish. We could see fish swimming around in the sparkling, clear blue water. This area is now known as Moomaw Lake and Gathrite Dam. We were catching all kinds of fish. I caught a twenty-three-inch fall fish, this is similar to a saltwater tarpon—large, silver, shiny scales. This is a bony fish. Most people don't eat them because of the hair like bones. We were catching nice bass, nothing really big. I noticed crawfish along the shoreline; I got out of the boat in search of catching them for bait. I caught a couple and returned to the boat. I gave one to Carl; he cast into swift-running water at the head of a deep hole. It no more than hit the water and something grabbed it; off it ran, Carl feeding him some line and then jerking as the line tightened up. Wow, a huge bass, about two feet, broke water. The fight was on. Carl fought him for about five minutes, being careful the reel was set just right. He landed the bass with the help of a net; it was a nice twenty-two-inch smallmouth, rather rare for our cold climate. I released the hook and lifted the bass from the net. Not thinking, I laid the bass on the seat beside Carl. He was bragging of what a nice one when the fish flipped, and over the side it went, back into the stream. Carl looked at me and said, "Hankie, I am going to kill you; you laid my fish there on purpose." I thought he was going to throw me out of the boat. I tried explaining it was a mistake. He said, "You ==, it was." I told him, "I will be your witness to the big catch. Now that you know a big one is here, it will be more fun catching him again." I guess you could say Carl started the first catch and release. As we continued fishing, Carl caught another big one, about twenty inches. After landing and securing it on a stringer, he turned to me and said, "Hankie, do we have anymore crawfish? I smiled and said, "No, but I can catch you some." Well, all was forgiven. Carl went home happy; he also knew of another good bait: crawfish. (They were my secret weapon. I learned this from my dad—my biggest fish a 5¼-pounder with a crawfish.)

On this job I worked forty hours a week. They had bleach plant foremen fill in on the same job and work forty to sixty hours a week. When they hired me it was on a sixty-day trial basis. That's why I worked overtime extras, to get a good rating. You could join the union after that. There are people that spend time looking into others' business. One of such people (a union rep) contacted me, asking if the transfer of lime was my job. I replied yes. He asked, "Were you offered the overtime, or did you refuse it?" I answered that I was not offered the overtime. (I guess someone was envious of others getting overtime.) He said, "According to the hours they worked, it is an equivalent of five hundred hours. You are entitled to recover that much pay at a time-and-a-half hourly rate; that would be $877." He talked me into filing a grievance against the company for that amount. About a week later two company officials contacted me in regard to the grievance. They shook hands, introducing themselves. (I knew their positions and names.) Grey E. said, "Hampton we have words that you are doing a fantastic job; however, we also have a signed grievance by you. How long have you been working for us?" I replied, "Sixty-four days." He replied, "Are you aware you are on a ninety-day trial basis? You have an honest complaint; however, we will pay for the loss of wages, but you will be terminated within the ninety-day period." I thought for a second and asked if I could see the papers. Immediately I ripped them up and put them in a trash can. Grey and Kahoon smiled, patted me on the back, and said, "Hamp, I think you made a wise decision. You will be remembered." I continued on that job. One day Grey E. came to me and asked, "How would you like to work in the bleach plant laboratory while the vacations are being taken?" I was thrilled and delighted. (He remembered me.) This was a daylight job. It was clean, and I didn't have to wear work clothes. I could also fill in for overtime on the other jobs.

I was self-trained in procedures just from reading the test procedures; however, it did not explain the details of the test. One test was on caustic. I placed the pipette into the sample, and I was supposed to put a squeeze bulb on the pipette for drawing up the solution. Big mistake, I placed my lips on the pipette as to use a straw. The end went into sludge on the bottom; pulling up on it, I got a mouthful of caustic. Wow, the skin on my lips, mouth, and tongue began to slit; it was like grease. I quickly washed my mouth, and seeing a vinegar bottle I washed my mouth. Spitting it out, black skin particles came out. (I remembered from Grandma's.) The burning was gone. I reported it; they sent me to the first aid for an examination—nothing serious, just rinse twice a day until better. When I returned we had a meeting, and they told us the seriousness of not completely following procedures; they also explained the domino effect. I tried thinking before actions. I must be careful.

Management (Grey E.) sent me to the chalk plant lab to fill in for vacations. This was another good job, only white dust of chalk in some areas. I tested the various tests in chalk before going to the customers. The main test was moisture and viscosity. Each customer had its own specifications; tests were done to these specs. The chalk was used for toothpaste and medicines, both liquids and pills. Some of the customers were E. R. Squibb, Bayer, Johnson and Johnson, and recreational departments. I worked shift work. When on eleven to seven I also went to the bleach plant lab and filled in for the seven to three shift.

I was given the opportunity to learn various positions. The next work area was the absorbers, that is where the lime was turned into chalk. We had a test using a mixture of alcohol and phenophinaline. When testing, it changed from pink to white as the chalk was completed.

When manufacturing chalk CO_2 gases passed through the absorber, blending with raw lime caused it to turn to chalk. The chalk was dried in a huge oven, similar to baking bread. At the other end, the chalk was bagged according to customer specifications, mostly fifty pounds. It was shipped to various customers—E. R. Squibb, Bristol Myers, and various manufacturers of toothpaste, Tums, Milk of Magnesia, Aspirin, and Maalox, and to a lot of medical and makeup corporations. I worked at this job until an opening came in the stores department. This area I was responsible for ordering and keeping on hand the needs for all the paper mill departments, and distributing them as needed. For me this would be a fulltime job; I would not fill in on other jobs in the company. Here I had a chance for promotions within the department, and all areas would be daylight seven to three except store clerks.

While I was working overtime, we were able to save enough money to start construction on a twenty-four-by-twenty-four-foot garage. I sold my service cycle for enough to buy two lots in Interval from dad. I worked with Mr. King at the chalk plant; he had a drilling machine. He drilled us a one hundred foot well for three dollars a foot including the needed casing. Betty was a worker; she helped me dig a three hundred foot septic line (in slate); also, we dug a four-by-eight-by-six-foot septic tank area. This was not an easy job. The garage was completed; it had a bath enclosed in one corner, a double sink attached to the wall, a washing machine and refrigerator, but no dryer. Clothes were hung outside to dry. Betty covered the area of the garage door with draperies. A sofa bed was fitted against the door, along with draperies. We had bunk beds for the children and a warm morning coal stove to provide heat. Betty had it looking like a dollhouse; this was similar to Aunt Nell's great kitchen. This was a great room the beginning of our great house. The reason for building the garage was that we wanted another baby. It would be too busy continuing to live at Mom and Dad's. We wanted out on our own.

At this time we were still living at Mom and Dad's.

Betty had our first daughter. Dr. Johnson and Betty had a bad time with the delivery. Betty having a deformed pelvis caused a problem birthing Deborah. Dr. Johnson was about to lose Betty and the baby; the baby's shoulders were causing the problem. Finally, without any additional help, the doctor finished the delivery. Betty was partly paralyzed on one side; the baby was healthy and beautiful, with black, curly hair that later turned blonde. Thanks to God and Dr. Johnson's talents, both were okay. We moved into the garage, it was great living there with the children. We immediately began construction on the basement of the house. The basement was finished, and we stopping further work (lack of finances). Dad confronted Betty and me with the offer of lending us the necessary money for completing the house. The agreement was that at completion we would borrow from the bank and repay Dad. This was great; we finished the house in eighteen months. It had a full basement with rec room and fireplace, all natural flooring and trim, and a fireplace upstairs with a raised hearth.

We borrowed $9,500 to pay Dad. Our total expense was $12,500. We heated the house with a coal furnace, using only $95 of coal for the winter (nine tons). Our transportation was an old 1936 Chevrolet; gasoline was only twenty-seven cents a gallon, and we could hardly afford that.

In addition, we were going to have another baby. I do not know why all these babies; it must be the well water.

When reporting for my first day at the stores department I was a laborer stocking inventory. This was a job where items were stocked until needed. After months on this job, I was promoted to junior clerk. This is where you approve and sign incoming orders. It is a desk job with a lot of signing; we did not have computers at that time. This was a neat job; you could not have an accident if you tried. My next position was maintaining and issuing oil as needed through the plant (you could get hurt here). The oil was delivered in fifty-five-gallon drums. In some areas, you only drew out portions from the drum. Another part of this job was issuing gasoline for the trucking department; this was done in the afternoon. I felt secure on this job; however, I was low in seniority, mill-wide.

The plant encountered a layoff of several positions. They laid off until I was the lowest in seniority; someone with more seniority than me pulled my job, and being the lowest, I had nowhere to pull. I would be without a job within a week.

I heard about an opening in the experimental pulp mill. This was a salary job, and you could not be pulled because of seniority. It also paid for overtime work. If you were off sick, you got your full pay. A week before my layoff I went to several executives in hopes of getting the E.P.M. job. I went to Mr. Voriss, who ran the E.O.M. facility. He was out of town; however, I talked to his wife. I explained my unfortunate layoff and that I had two children and one on the way, also that Deborah was in the hospital from a freak bathtub accident. I also explained about just moving into a house, and our payment was $127 a month. She was very understanding, having children of their own and having just completed their home. Not knowing that this would have any influence, I decided to go to Mr. Hooks. He was the superintendent of that end of the plant. I also explained the situation to him. He was a friend of my dad's; Dad worked as a supervisor under his jurisdiction. I told him I could not afford to be laid off. I asked if he would check my work records and supervisors, for accountability. It was now left up to a prayer being answered. The next day my supervisor, Mr. Mcdonald, asked me to report to the personnel department and take a test. Well, I'm not the brightest egg in the carton. I did not know how this would go, especially under pressure. Mr. Mc. came by and said that I did okay on the test and that they would call me. Thanks to answers and some caring people, I now had a job at the e.p.m. at a salary of $300 a month. This was a shift work job; however, I did not mind. I was working.

The e.p.m. pilot plant was for pulp improvement on brightness cost versus yield.

It involved seven stages of processing, starting at chipping logs (pulpwood), cooking the chips, screening, chlorination, caustic extraction, washing the pulp, and high-density bleaching. My first position was the laboratory—cooking, brightness, consistency, and chemical reaction. Tests were made every hour.

While working I encountered all employees. It was like a big family; we cooked our meals on each shift. We had a refrigerator for keeping our foods. Byers, (our supervisor) daily brought in a quart of milk. Byrne, a coworker, would drink out of Byer's container. Byers got ticked off. He brought in a new quart, opened it in front of Byrne, took a drink, then spat in it, and said, "Byrne, this is my—milk. Byrne went over, picked up the container, took a drink, spat in it, and said, "Byers, this is our—milk. Now, that takes a lot of brass. Byers hid his milk location. The next story is on Byrne and Squirrel.

On another day it was payback for Squirrel. He and Byrne were at each other. Squirrel was in the bathroom sitting on the commode. Byrne slipped in with a pressure bulb and a pipette filled with acetone. Seeing Squirrel on the commode, he squirted the fluid around his feet and threw in a lighted match; it caused a sudden flame. With such a surprise, Squirrel lifted his feet as if to stand on the commode. Byrne, catching him in this position, went higher with the flame. Squirrel stood up with his trousers around his ankles. As he reached for the top of the enclosure, the flames were licking at his rear end; his pants fell down, with his bare rear end showing. He landed on the other side, kicking and swearing. Well, this was a real payback. At this they drew a truce.

As we finished our tower, everyone tried to beat each other out of the parking lot. Earlier we went down and jacked the rear end of Squirrel's car up one-fourth of an inch. He reached his car about the same time as some of the others. He started the engine, raced the motor, and popped the clutch, and the car just rocked a little, no movement. Then he put it in reverse and did the same; again, nothing happened. He jumped out of the car and walked around the car trying to find the problem; he noticed nothing. Again he duplicated the previous actions. Everyone was parked at the other end of the parking lot having a big laugh. Squirrel got out of the car and kicked the tire, and the wheel turned a little. He was furious;

for a little guy, he made a big noise. Everyone decided to cool it with Squirrel; he was a good sport.

My next position was the bleach plant. In this area, pulp and chemicals were weighed, and at the beginning and end of a successful eight-hour continuous run was required for a qualification of completion.

Tests were made at every stage of bleaching. To get on specs sooner, I tested every fifteen minutes, making adjustments until on test, then changed to every thirty minutes to ensure proper specs. We were required to test every hour. Pulp traveled from a blending tank to a pretension tower, where bleach was added. It then went to caustic extraction, from chlorinator there, to the Oliver. where it was washed. One day as I was cleaning around the washer (Oliver), I shut the switch box down. Accidentally, I hosed down the electrical box. When trying to restore the current, there was a sizzling jet sound. I shut the switch down. I knew what the problem was, and I just wanted to get a reaction from Byers, our foreman. When having problems I summoned him.

I went to Byers and said, "I have an electrical problem with the Oliver table. I didn't tell him the electrical box was wet; I wiped the water from it. He said, "Forbes you just don't know what you are doing. Pull the switch down and hold it." We walked to the panel box. I hung back a little and stepped to one side, not knowing what might happen. The floor was wet. Byers slammed down the switch handle and held it. Wow, fire came from the panel, flashing by his head and dancing off the framework of the Oliver. He looked like death—his hair standing high on his head. He said, "Forbes, what the devil have you done? You could have killed me." Trying not to laugh, I turned my head and walked away. When I contained myself I said, "I'm sorry. I was a little reckless." I let this incident cool down before trying anything else.

We were enjoying our home; the children were comfortable with it. Betty was constantly cleaning and waxing, and it was spick-and-span. She was a great decorator; this was a special gift. There wasn't anything she couldn't do. She didn't have a driver's license; however, she mastered that old '36 Chevrolet, straight gears and all. Betty was expecting Therressa. She was born in the old Alleghany Memorial Hospital, a fine healthy 8¾-pound girl. Dr. Johnson was Betty's doctor; however, Dr. Jamison delivered Therressa. Dr Johnson quit delivering babies after the difficult time he had with Betty and Deborah. This was a great loss for the neighborhood. Betty was a great mother, being only twenty.

Money was still tight. I only made $300 a month, and our house payment was $125. We were conservative in all areas; Betty made the children's clothes and most of her clothing.

Dad decided to start a storm window business; we called it Hamp and Hank.

Once a month I got a four-day break, plus other off days. I had plenty of time for selling. (I would not advise anyone to do this; it took prime time away from Betty and the children.)

Sales were great; we made a good profit. Now we could afford a good car. We purchased a station wagon (Ford). It was good for the business and the growing family. Later we added carports, utility rooms, wrought iron railings, and awnings. We hired two people as installers.

The extra money was used so as to have nicer things for the children and to give Betty a break.

We needed some kind of advertisement for the business. We purchased a Crosley (small car) from a friend. We had storm windows, our phone numbers, and "Hamp" and "Hank" on each side. It worked well for advertising the business. I drove it everywhere on window business. It was parked at each sales location during installation. I added ladder racks and carried a ladder for measuring window sales. We got a lot of comments and calls concerning the business.

One day the car stopped running; it seemed not to be getting gasoline. It had plenty of gasoline in the tank. I decided to remove the carburetor; there was a fine hair filter. It was a mass of tiny hairs. Cautiously I removed the substance; it wasn't a filter, just a mass. I removed the fuel line; there was the same substance within. I removed the line going to the tank and a cup of fuel, with the same substance. It really puzzled me. Later I found the remains of a cattail stem in the line. This was the work of my son, Hampton III. He was using the cattails as a torch; it was his method of gassing the torch. I didn't punish him. I just said, "Oh, not another one." Needles to say, the Crosley never ran again.

On another occasion he was setting grass fires and riding in from the highway with some of my firefighter friends; that's where the nickname Bug came from.

Today I am working the seven to three shift. It is nice; you have mornings off. Also, there are no management teams around. On this day I started in on the Oliver washer, the pulp would go into another retention (two hours) tower, where chemicals and heat were applied. The pulp was then delivered to the washer, in front of the sodium hypochlorite tower. Here the pulp dropped in, applying steam and a sodium solution. The consistency has to be right to get a flow into the tower, instead of a stacking effect. This was a problem area for plugging up. On one occasion I was having a problem with plugging up.

Steam was building up within, creating a pressure pocket. Usually this could be corrected using a long rod, pushing it through the top crust and allowing the top pulp to collapse and fall. With the condition perfect for a blowback. Not taking any chances, I decided to call on my buddy. I went to Byers for support. "Byers," I said, "I have a plug up, the hippo tower." He replied, "You and your problems. Let me show you the secret in solving this simple problem." On one end of the building there was a two-story wall; it was about fifty feet away. Byers went to the problem area. Again I stood off to one side. He picked up the pole and began driving it through the plugged area for about five minutes with no effect. Finally he drove the rod down, working it back and forth. I shut the feed down so nothing would pile up.

All at once a relief hole was made, and about a ton of pulp blew out of the tower. Byers was in the way and took the main part of the blow. The remaining pulp going by went to the wall on the opposite end of the building. There was a void in the center of the wall that looked like the outline of a giant man. Byers turned, looking like a snowman. He said, "Forbes, from now on fix. Your own—problems. I had to laugh. The image on the wall was from the pulp he caught. Well, I had a lot of pulp to clean up this day, and it had to be weighed and accounted for.

During my time at E.P.M. I experienced a lot. I was also aware of accident prevention. I worked with a lot of caring engineers. One such person was B. Bloom. He was a caring individual who wanted the most from your potential. He appreciated everything you did on the job. The e.p.m. was phasing out; the same accomplishments could result from a smaller-scale procedure. The date was set for the closure. One week prior to the shutdown, B. Bloom came to me and asked if I would be interested in a transfer to Product Development. I was delighted, and thanked him. I was scheduled for the interview. A friend, Keller, previously worked with me at e.p.m. He put in a good word for me. I was hired. It was a seven-and-one-half-hour day, starting at eight with a one-hour lunch, and leaving at four thirty. This was a great learning experience. Most people using paper or a paper cup have no idea how involved the product manufacturing and required testing can be. I will list some of my test duties: caliper, basis weight, density, bulk, weight per caliper point, tear, stretch, tensile strength, porosity, color, holdout oil ink, printing, score bend, mullion, porosity, vancometer, coffee holdout cobb, glue ability, tack, bond, coatings, and ash. This is a real learning experience of paper manufactoring. These are daily tests made on various paper reels as they come off the machine. Additional tests are made on cartons, bulge, crush, corner crush, volume, area, and smoothness. We spent time in the production area, to see the purpose of these tests, and also in customer plants, to see their operations and problems. I really liked this job, especially for the learning experiences.

When checking competitors' paper for a comparison to properties, I was required to make a duplicate carton with our paper according to the carton I was checking. In doing this I learned to make hand samples (cartons).

This was a plus. The company would eventually grow into a packaging converting business; they were the owners of Virginia Folding Box, a previous customer.

During this time, yes, we had another baby girl Gwyneth. She was a lovely baby with blushed skin and red (strawberry), curly hair. Again Mom was proud we had another redhead. Betty was like a protective hen; she loved her children. She was like a kid herself when it came to playing with them.

Another job-related responsibility was cutting customer samples to a given sheet size for testing. This was done on a guillotine. Standard sheet sizes were used from which to cut the proper size. The stock (paper) was placed under the knife and cut on four sides to the required size. I was cutting an order. I had made two cuts. You would cut, then rotate the slug of paper and cut the opposite side. It was a very safe procedure. You have both hands on a double starter button beneath the cutter. After finishing the third cut, I was reaching for the slug of paper, with both hands about six inches away. Suddenly the knife began a continuous chopping action. I jumped back, the hair on my neck standing. I began to gag, thinking of what could have happened. I could have lost both hands. (Dad always said to me, "You make your living with those hands.") The electrical panel shorted out. They flagged the cutter and worked on it about two weeks. From then on, when samples needed to be cut I was busy doing other projects.

We continuously made competitive analyses on competitors' paper products cartons. I enjoyed this; it gave me continuous experience in making hand samples. I soon became a skilled sample maker.

Virginia Folding Box used a large tonnage of paperboard for the flip-top cigarette carton. We often visited the Richmond plant, checking on the run ability of the board. I grew in knowledge of carton converting and in fondness of the procedure. I also participated in carton design.

CHAPTER V

Delaware Era

THE COMPANY WAS expanding in the area of packaging. They were building a manufacturing facility in Newark, Delaware, for the production of carton converting. An opening came for carton engineer; they offered me the job. After consulting Betty, I accepted the position. This was quite a challenge,

It meant leaving our families and friends. Also, it meant selling our home and relocating. There was a lot of preparation for the move.

First I wanted to get rid of my worldly living and start obeying God, with thanks for my success. Living in a new place, walking in newness, that may take awhile, but it would happen.

We were trying to sell our house for $16,500. This would give us a marginal profit. Higgins, father-in-law, lived next door. He was helping me with work around the house. I said to him, "We are going to sell the house for $16,500 at 5 percent interest on a 360-month payment plan, no down payment." Checking with the bank, the payment would be $102. He didn't show any interest; however, that night he called and said, "Are you serious about your home proposal?" I said, "Positive." Both families agreed, and the sale was made. It was sold on a land contract, with no transfer of title. He could not borrow or make changes. If he borrowed, he had to pay the note off. He would deposit the monthly payment into my bank account. I still owed on the house. I deposited $23 to the account, and it made our monthly payment.

I went to Newark, Delaware, to check the work situation and the housing availability.

The converting plant was under construction. Offices were set up in Newark for a temporary working area. Newark was a small college town—the University of Delaware.

The housing market was plentiful, with new construction within a twenty-mile radius. I couldn't afford an older house; the down payment was too high. The newer houses were $2,000 down plus closing. I searched about ten builders, crawling in and out of the construction and checking out the quality of materials and labor. I met Mr. Marta, a builder in the area. He was at North Wilmington. He asked me to check out another of his sites, Eastburn Acres, which was within six miles of my work area. I was familiar with this project; it was my choice site. At this location I was checking out a brick rancher similar to the one we sold. We needed four bedrooms, so I decided to further examine a bilevel construction. This construction offered four bedrooms, two baths, two garages. and a rec room, plus living, dining, and kitchen. It was exactly what we needed for the size of our family. Marta was an understanding gentleman. I told him my situation. I was interested in the house; however, I didn't have a down payment at that time. I would have it within a week, on my next trip. He shook hands, saying, "See you next week."

Westvaco was paying my expenses. I caught the train for home. I explained the conditions to Dad, and he financed the down payment. I was to repay him later. I didn't explain this deal to Betty. I just said I looked at numerous houses, and most were suitable for our needs.

I rented a room at the Deer Park Hotel; it was also a bar and dining area, a hangout for college students.

Returning to Wilmington, I caught the C & O train; it had a sleeper. This was great. I could wake up in Wilmington. I explained to the porter to wake me before entering the Wilmington station—big mistake. When I woke up he was announcing arriving at the Wilmington station. Hurriedly I put my shirt on, pants around my knees, and running for the exit—pants down, shoes and bag in hand. I just made it. I was getting off as the train departed. This was the first time I dressed on a station platform. As Ronald Reagan would say, "Here we go again." I reported for work in a shook-up mood.

At the office I met Chuck, who was employed because of his background in sample making. He was quite a character; he also had a vast knowledge in corrugated containers. He was only in town one day, and I think he knew everyone important. He was a big spender, with or without money. I picked up some knowledge from him and vice versa. We worked well together.

That afternoon I placed the down payment on the house; all we lacked was Betty's signature. Within a week I brought Betty to Newark to check out the location and available housing. I shouldn't have done it; however, I took her to every location I had previously checked out. By the end of the day she was disgusted with houses and their locations. Then I took her to Eastburn Acres. She knew nothing about the previous decision. We went to the exact house I put a deposit on. She liked the area; it was halfway between Wilmington and Newark. Entering the house, she began looking around. By the end of the tour, she had an imaginary idea of the location of all our furniture. She said, "This is an ideal house. Why don't you consider this one?" I replied, "It is sold." She had a look to kill on her face. Seeing she was a little disgusted, I said, "We are the owners." She was happy but peeved. She said, "Why did you waste my day showing me all those other houses?" Betty measured the windows, returned home, and made draperies for all windows and doors. We packed everything according to room locations, and the movers loaded and were on their way to Delaware. When arriving, Betty supervised the unloading—everything in its location in every room. When the movers left, the house looked like a sample home, with everything in place, and even draperied.

We brought the children to their new home. They were delighted, each having his or her own bedroom, and a park two doors down. Within a week they were in school and found new friends.

Our car wasn't much. I decided to buy a Buick station wagon with three rows of seats. Everyone could ride shotgun. This made it possible to go home on weekends.

The first responsibility was finding a church. Betty went to various denominations, choosing Cedars Church of Christ. Not living in newness after my first baptism, I decided to rededicate and be baptized again.

One day when coming home from work, a group of children was hanging out front. Pat was sitting on a minibike. He said, "Mr. Forbes, would you like to take a ride on my bike?" I was familiar with motorbikes and service cycles. After a little persuasion, I accepted his offer. I got on that bike and opened the throttle. It stuck on wide open; the front end lifted up, and I was riding on one wheel for a time. I tried braking it. No help. All at once it began to rise even more; it flipped backward. My butt hit the pavement, sliding for five feet. When coming to a stop, the bike was twenty-five feet, ahead of me on its side, running wide open in a circle. They helped me up. I felt a little breeze around my butt, the whole rear end of my trousers was missing. I said, "That thing will kill you. Pat said, "Mr. Forbes, I forgot to tell you the gas sticks." That was the end of minibike rides. I changed clothes and went back to work.

The converting plant was finally finished. We relocated; we were in a large office with drafting tables and an area for cutting hand samples.

Our job was completing sales customer needs; this involved designing and making hand samples for customer approvals. As we increased our sales force, we had more sales requests. We put on two more draftsmen.

The draftsmen were Buddy and Andy. I trained both to make hand samples. Both caught on and completed the requests given them. Buddy became quite a good designer; he was worth a lot more than he was being paid. He was also a good artist. The method of making hand samples was drawing out the carton style in two dimensions, stapling three sheets of paperboard together, and pinholing with a needle the ends of where the scores were. The samples were cut by hand on straight cuts, and with curved knives for radius. You ended up with three blank samples; then the creases (folding areas) were applied. We ended up with three samples—one for the customer, one for estimating, and one for the file. This procedure was later replaced with a cad cam computer for drafting and a computer method for cutting and creasing. This saved a lot of time and produced a greater number of cartons.

In time I was made design supervisor, in charge of samples, design, dies, and sample orders.

One afternoon on the way home it was sprinkling rain. I removed my glasses and laid them on the seat until I had a chance to clean them. As I drove along it started raining harder. I noticed a person thumbing. He was getting wet. Like a good Samaritan, I stopped and picked him up. I listened to his hardships, then gave him a couple dollars for food. He was very thankful. I let him out at the stop light where I was turning. I pulled into the driveway, parked, and began looking for my glasses. To my surprise, he had sat on my glasses. One lens was broken, and the frames were bent up like pretzels. It pays to keep your glasses on, or don't pick up hikers.

That reminds me of another day. I was driving up Kirkwood Highway. A college student was thumbing; she was neatly dressed and was carrying a backpack. I picked her up. After driving a mile she asked, "Mind if I smoke?" Thinking no harm, I said okay. She went into her neatly organized bag and pulled out a smoke. She lit it up and, wow, it smelled like a hay field burning. Looking a little closer, it was hand rolled. Here I was with an underage girl in my car with a joint. I said, "What are you smoking?" She said, "Just a joint." Betty had warned me about picking up unknowns. I let her out before my destination. Home I went with the windows down.

During this time, money was still tight. There were hidden costs not considered. I had relocated. Phone bills were greater, insurances was higher, food cost were higher, transportation cost were greater, and even utilities were higher. I decided to do a part-time job selling and installing storm windows and doors. My friend Jim from e.p.m. and his family also transferred to Delaware. We were working in the same plant.

I would sell during the week and some Saturdays. Jim and I would install. **This worked well for both of us; we were both making extra money. On one job we were** installing windows at ground level. I extended myself. I was standing on the extreme top of the ladder reaching the top window screws. The back side of the ladder was on the ground. Jim, wanting to help me with the lower screws, stepped onto the ladder on the opposite side.

It sank about six inches into the soft ground. Before I realized what was happening, I went sailing through the air, my arms swinging, trying not to land on my back. I got up with a dizzy head and said, "Jim, you finish the job." With a slight smile Jim repositioned the ladder and completed the job; later we had a good laugh.

The next weekend I was installing doors for my boss (Dudley). I was installing for about six hours. I had an unusual feeling as if something was wrong. I completed the job and went home. I said to Betty, "I have had a weird feeling all day." Betty looked at me with a smirk. She said, "Look at your shoes." I looked down and could not believe what I saw. I did a double take. I had on a plain toe and a wing tip. Dudley later gave me a window order; I guess he felt sorry for my footwear and thought I needed the money. I was hoping for a raise.

One weekend I drove to Covington to drive Tex (my brother in-law) up for some time. As we were traveling Route 81 the traffic was bad, with tractor trailers. I decided to take Route 11 for a break. As we were traveling toward Edinburg, Virginia, we saw two turkeys running along a fence on the side of the highway. I had my bow in the car from a previous deer hunt. I pulled off the road and got out of the car with bow and arrow in hand. As the turkeys were searching for a hole in the fence, I drew the bow, took aim, and a turkey was flopping. The other one went through the fence to safety. I picked up the turkey and put it in the back of the station wagon. I would dress and clean the turkey when I got back on Route 81. After about two miles we both began to scratch. Checking my arms, I discovered lice. That turkey infested the interior with lice. We thought we were going to get eatten up before we came to a pull-off leading to the river. We got out with the turkey and opened all doors in order to air out the fleas. I skinned and dressed the turkey, put it in the cooler, and hoped the fleas had escaped. As we drove, we imagined flea bites all the way home, a most uncomfortable experience. By the way, those turkeys were tame; they escaped from a truck headed for a Tyson processing facility.

This is another bird story. The family drove toward Rock Hall to perch fish. As we were driving we noticed thousands of geese feeding in the cornfields. We drove to a location where there was a pool of water below a dam waterfall. Here we caught yellow perch on every cast. The fish were running and could not get beyond this point. This became a favorite place for March; we often brought friends and family to this area. We love fishing and sports. You can take the boy out of the country but not the country out of the boy. On the return home the geese were still feeding in the cornfields. I had an idea. Those birds were heavy from all that corn. I thought I could outrun them, catching them before they took flight. Well, the race was on. I ran like a racehorse toward the center of the flock; geese were flapping their wings and running in every direction. I was gaining on them; some were taking off. Others continued to run. Finally I overtook one, flopping and kicking. I managed to capture it. The backseat had a well in the floorboard. I placed the goose in it and folded the seat over. It was confined, just a quack or two on the way home. We unloaded the car and prepared a place to clean the fish. The children were excited, saying, Get the goose. Get the goose. What are we going to do with it?" Cautiously I lifted the seat, secured the bird, and lifted it out. Wow, I now know what they mean when saying "crap like a goose." That well was filled with goose crap; it must have been five pounds. I put the goose under a basket and began to clean out that mess. I had to hose the area—not a good idea. The kids and I carried the goose to the school playground and released it; it hung around for a while, I guess to get its bearings, and running for a while it took off into the wild blue yonder. The kids were happy about the release. They said, "We can catch him another time." Another bad idea. Live and learn, or live and never learn.

Betty had a job at J. C. Penney. On our way to work I picked up Buddy. We drove to the shopping center, where I dropped off Betty. We had had a blowing snow that night, and there were snowdrifts. As we were leaving the area, a big, deep snowdrift was ahead of us. I stopped, hesitating whether to turn and go back, or charge the drift. Buddy was somewhat of a daredevil. He said, "Back up, get a running start, and hit the center." Well, Evel Knievel, here we go. I hit the drift; it was glazed with ice. We went halfway upon the drift, and the car sunk down a foot. Here we were two feet of the ground, unable to get the doors open. We put pressure on the door back and forth until we got an opening large enough to squeeze through. Out we went. We had a lot of snow to move, three feet high and ten feet long. We acquired shovels and began to make a path in front of the car; I knew we were going to be late this day. Finally, after an hour, we were on our way to work. I think Buddy liked the excitement better than work. Needless to say, we had an excuse for tardiness.

The children were out front playing. I was unaware the keys were in the car. We were out at the time. Debby was not the brave one; however, she started the car while it was parked in front of the two garage doors; she began backing up and going forward. Therressa, being braver, got on the front fender, enjoying the ride. After a while she got off. Debby continued her driving. All at once she hit the gas too hard; the car went into the post separating the garage doors. Both garage doors were destroyed, and the center post (holding up the house) was pushed in at the base.

When I got home, the children were scared to death. After examining the damage I talked to Debby about her actions. She volunteered the truth. I couldn't punish her; I was happy no one was hurt. I told the children if they told the truth they wouldn't be punished. All was not lost. I got an estimate, and the insurance paid for labor and materials. I borrowed a jack from the fire company, jacked the house up in the area of the post, and drove the post back into place using a sledgehammer. Instead of hiring someone for the repairs, I decided to do the job myself. I had an idea not to replace the garage doors. I closed in the top area with two windows on each side of the post. The base was enclosed with framing and stucco to match the foundation. On the interior I built a bar with refrigerator, paneling on the walls, and bookshelves on the end. Everything was rustic. I built a cross-buck door entering the laundry room. I used scrap lumber from skids (oak), cutting groves in it to form squares for the bar and trim.

The children now had their own recreation room. All their friends enjoyed it. Betty got a pool table from the Salvation Army, and this was the finishing touch. Just remember, something good from something bad.

Sometime later, returning from work, Therressa met me at the door. There was glass all around. She, with a slight smile, said, "Daddy, I broke the door." Not giving her a chance to explain, I spanked her with my hand. She whimpered a little and said, "You told us if we told the truth you wouldn't punish us. With this, I gave her a hug and apologized. I was in the wrong. I felt like a heel for making this mistake; I really violated her trust.

Be careful of what you promise. Children don't forget.

We were in Covington on another weekend. I noticed a 1964½ fastback (Ford) Mustang, red with racing stripes. Betty liked fast cars, and this was a winner. We purchased it and drove to Newark. Everyone loved it. Weeks later Betty had a previous speeding warning, the same officer caught her speeding at Bay Bridge on the way to Richmond. He said, "I don't want to give you a ticket; however, I will follow you for the next ten miles. If you go one mile over the limit, I will take your driving permit." She now has a light foot.

Our son, Hampton III, was nicknamed Bug; this name was given when we lived in Interval. As a youngster he was fascinated with matches and fire. There was a lot of open land with tall grass and weeds; he constantly set fires. He knew the men in the fire department. He would walk to the entrance of the development and ride in on the fire truck with his friends. In order to stop this, we had a friend on the police force talk to him in lockup. Finally, scared, he graduated from setting fires.

He got his driver's license at sixteen; his next ambition was to drive the Mustang. After some begging and promising, Betty let him drive the car. About an hour later he came home with the keys. Betty said, "What have you done with the car?" He replied, "It was towed to the garage. I popped the clutch and shot the clutch. They said it should be replaced with a heavy-duty clutch." He was grounded for a while.

Like father like son. We had a grill on the back patio; I was fascinated with the spark that ignited the gas. After some thinking I decided to experiment with the flash from the starter button. I didn't understand from a friction push button how it created an arc, or electrical charge. Well, curiosity got the best of me. I pinched the area of the spark and pushed the button. Wow! Wow! The hair stood up on my head, and my fingers felt like a firecracker went off. What a sting. A hit with a hammer would have felt better. I should have looked it up on the Internet.

Another day I tightened up the valves on the control knobs of the grill. I was getting a gas smell, not thinking the nut could be cross-threaded.

I decided to check the leak. (I knew better; while at work we used soap bubbles.) I turned the gas on. I began to detect an odor and sound. With a flashlight I checked to see the leak area. Gas still leaking, I hit the ignition button—big mistake. I had an explosion. Picking up the parts, I junked the grill. Never check for a leak with a flame.

I went to Covington every chance I got. If I had $20 and a full tank of gasoline, I took off. Gwyneth went with me on this occasion. I was driving Betty's Mustang. Knowing the mountain roads, I accepted a challenge by another driver. I was first at the top of the mountain. Going around a curve, I felt the clutch slip; later on it was because I touched the clutch. While in Covington I noticed a 1969 fastback. After checking it out—big mistake—I traded Betty's car. At home, she was not happy; later on, I was not happy. The car had a lot of problems. It vibrated because of tires and front-end problems. The windows when being rolled down would come out of the tracks and then fall in the channels. My boss at the carton plant was L. Lafrinier. I gave a moon party at his home. (It was large enough to accommodate a crowd.) The main menu was corn charcoaled in the shuck, along with hot dogs and hamburgers. We had a great party. When leaving, the car was steamed up, and I am not good at backing up. I hit a telephone pole, vibrating the hooked-up houses. I pulled up and backed safely into the road. At work the next morning Larry brought in a ten-pound bag with car parts. That car was plastic; we had it repaired and later sold it.

On another trip to Covington, I was going deer hunting. I was off for a week. Traveling alone you get very sleepy. I usually pull off and take a nap; however, this time I was fighting sleep. This was before the washboard effect along the edges of the road. I nodded a time or two but continued, thinking the sleepiness would pass—big mistake. I woke up in the gravel at 65 miles an hour with the horn blowing. The horn was located on the inside of the steering wheel; when going off the road I must have squeezed the steering wheel, causing the horn to blow. Well, that woke me up. I sat there for twenty minutes without going to sleep. Warning, the life you save could be your own.

Westvaco had a procedure; they had group hiring, twenty to thirty in a group. They would expose the group to every phase of the industry, as they observed each division they could determine what division they preferred to work in.

This was the part of my responsibilities I enjoyed most. I would create a show and tell using about twenty-five of my best designs. I would start with an introduction of each salesperson. The seminar would last about two hours or longer, depending on the interest. I would start by telling the history of the design—the customer, the product, and demonstrating how the design would be produced in manufacturing, side-seam glued or shipped flat to be formed on customer equipment. Also, I would show the product being loaded and the shelf displaying of product and carton. A lot of questions were asked. Who determined the design? Did we get customer input? I tried to answer all questions; it's a learning process. Designs were first, depending on customer needs. Whether machine formed and loaded or formed and loaded by hand, samples were made with economy in mind. On any given request, I would take everything into consideration. Usually I would make three or four designs. The customer would then have a choice of preference. If only one design was made, and the customer didn't like it, you were out unless he gave you another opportunity. If the customer picked a design, he may have input for some additional features to be incorporated.

The weather was changing from fall to winter; fuel prices both transportation and heating were increasing. We decided to purchase a wood-burning insert. We checked around for the styles and availability.

We decided on an Englander, a family-owned manufacturer company in Lynchburg Virginia. We purchased the stove and installed it on the hearth of the fireplace. The stove heated the house, and it was so efficient. It would burn overnight when fully loaded. After burning the stove, we decided to contact Mr. England for a franchise in Wilmington. The cost was only $500. We ordered a trailer-load of stoves. I rented a building in a shopping center near the house. We set up the shop with the stoves (twenty) chain saws, and Betty put in antiques. England stoves of Delaware was now in business. Betty kept the shop while I worked at the carton plant. She was a good salesman. From reading, she knew more about stoves than the manufacturer. On a good day she would sell five units. We had refrigerator trucks for moving the stoves around and a hydraulic lift for loading. Our display area cost $600 a month, plus another area for storage ($150). As time passed we would pick up special orders, if only six or eight. I rented a U-Haul on location; they loaded the order, and I was on the way to Delaware. After unloading the stoves at the shop, I returned the truck to a rental location. I had a passenger (helper) with me. As I pulled into the drop-off area, there was a row of parked cars. As I moved closer to the station I heard a c-r-u-n-c-h crunch. I said, "Now what?" I put the truck in reverse. As I was moving backward someone was waving his arms and hollering. I went about five more feet, and c-r-u-n-c-h, crunch again. The excited man was jumping three feet off the ground. I got out of the truck to see what the excitement was all about. Oh, no. I ran over the man's car hood. He was working on his car in the parking area. He said, "I hope you have insurance!"

I replied, "I'm not insured for running over hoods." I said, "From now on, park your hood in a standing position." Betty picked us up, and we returned to the shop. The business was growing, and we needed more space. We decided for the $750 a month we were spending, we would purchase a suitable property for housing sales and storage. We were spending a total of $867 for shop, storage, and house payment. We found a place on a major highway. It included a brick home and two garages on 7½ acres joining the University of Delaware's agriculture area of five hundred acres. The price was $117,000. We contacted the Realtor. We made a firm offer of $82,000. The Realtor was skeptic. He delivered the contract, explaining that we wouldn't pay higher. To our surprise, they accepted the offer with one request, that we released the $20,000 down payment in advance of closing. (They needed the money for the purchase of transportation.) The contract included that they would hold the mortgage at 5 percent. Our payment before was $867; our new payment was $560. We were in good shape. I quit the window business. Where there is a will, there is a way. God has been good to us. We sold the Eastburn Acres house for $49,000. The stove business gave us the incentive to take on a greater obligation.

In the afternoon (after work), I would work at home with Betty. The garages were used as a display shop for stoves, saws, antiques, and shrubbery for sale.

Betty let no grass grow under her feet. She started a garden center, selling shrubbery along with antiques. She purchased plants in New Jersey. The markup was three times the purchase price; she could sell one and plant two. She had four acres looking like Longwood Gardens. The other 3.5 acres were wooded, with a stream running through the property. The wooded area had deer, squirrels, rabbits, and quail. Betty went home for a visit.

While she was gone, I set up a deer stand in the bedroom. Deer were feeding in the yard. That evening about dust they came though. I had the window up and waiting. I picked off one with the first shot. I hung and skinned the animal, cutting it up and placing it in the freezer. I went back to the area of the bedroom and, watching television, waited patiently for another one. I nodded off, and when looking out the window I saw two white legs, I took a second look, and it looked bigger. I placed the gun out the window, sighted in, and was ready to pull the trigger when I noticed another set of legs, and then a flat top. Wow, I was about to shoot up Betty's laced white cast iron table. To prevent a problem, I went to bed. The next morning I went to work.

When I returned home from work, Betty was there. She was in a good mood after her family visit; she fussed a little because the bedroom was out of order.

We continued working on the property in our spare time. The property had a two-hundred-yard driveway. On one side was a row of dead pine trees every fifteen feet, mingled with brush, grapevines, and ivies. I cleaned between the trees. I planted rhododendron, and we were going to plant flowering cherries when the pines were removed. It was quite windy, being on the crest of the hill. A tornado-force wind blew down some of the pines. One tree about sixteen inches in diameter fell across a cable that leads to the highway. The top limbs were touching a hot wire, causing a spark and flame until the end burned off. The trunk of the tree was hanging on a cable under the hot wire. The wire was drooped about two feet, from the weight of the fallen tree (kind of like a bow). I placed a ladder on the cable and secured it. I started up my Poulan saw, and up the ladder I went. I began to saw about ten feet of the tree trunk off. When releasing the weight from the cable, I sprung the ladder up, and I went about five feet above the cable (like a human arrow), saw still running and in my hand. I don't remember hitting the ground. When I woke up, the saw was beside me, running. Dizzy and confused, I looked myself over. No blood. I then looked around to see if anyone was watching. Later we cleared the dead trees and planted fifteen-foot cherry trees. They were beautiful.

At the stove shop we had cords of stacked wood. We used one of the stoves to heat the building. I noticed some of the wood was missing. After about a week I decided to drill and poured gun powder in two of the logs. I put a plug in to make it tight, hoping the thief burns the wood—big mistake. Then someone rearranged the wood, and I lost the location of the powdered wood. I continued to use from the pile. One afternoon just before closing I loaded up the stove for an overnight burn. An hour later I was preparing to close, when it sounded like dynamite going off. I am glad I wasn't in front of the stove door; it blew open, with sparks flying. Luckily there were no customers. I was afraid to use or sell from that pile of wood. I think someone reversed my scheme.

We were having problems with rats boring holes under the cement porch. The place was becoming a mess. I had an idea. I watched the area and, sure enough, an old mother rat and two siblings were playing around the hole. I got the gas can used for the chain saw and emptied it into the cavity, then moved the can to another location. As I stood over the area, I dropped a lit match in the hole. Wow, fire flew out of the area like a flamethrower. The ground shook, and my knees buckled from the shock. Everyone in the next building came running. I said, "No problem. It's just the exterminator." Sam the barber cut his customer while shaving him. Luckily, it didn't crack the cement. I was thankful for that.

We had three barrels we used for burning trash in a nearby lot. We placed corrugated and other material on the stack. As usual, I lit the corrugated, and the trash began to burn. I don't know what caused all the smoke; the lot and highway were filled with smoke. Well, more excitement. Someone called the fire department, thinking the trailer park behind us was on fire. We had a lot of excitement—a five-alarm fire, with trucks everywhere. We had a fire truck parade in the parking lot. It was legal to burn trash at a distance from a business. I was lucky on the correct distance. I was warned not to have such a large fire.

While living in Eastburn Acres there was a boxer that just loved our trash can. It was a large paper sack placed on a metal rack with a cover. Daily when making his rounds we were number one on the program. Well, getting tired of picking up trash and losing trash bags, I decided to take action. I placed a bale of hay on each side of the runway to the trash can. I placed a metal rack in the center with a foam insulator at ground level. I placed a duplicate rack in front of the raised one. I hooked two ends from an extension cord on each rack; I plugged the extension cord into the current. We had a picture window above the trash can, a perfect view of what was to take place. The timing was just right for that boxer's arrival. Well, here he came walking a little stiff-legged, with his chest stuck out. Noticing something wasn't right, he paused for a minute. Temptation got the best of him; upon those racks he went. I have never heard a dog make such a sound. The shock kicked him back about ten feet under a bush. Dazed, he staggered to his feet. still squalling, he staggered off. I decided to check out his route the next morning. I sat on the front steps. Here he came with that strut. Before reaching our location he crossed the street, veering away from our trash can. Needless to say, the trash problem was solved.

On one occasion I left a stove on a cart outside the shop. We had a three-wheel bike, and I decide I needed the exercise. I got on the bike, riding toward the shop. About halfway there the tire on the back right blew. Here I was, no transportation. I decided to try something, I leaned the bike over, similar to a dog holding up one leg. Off I went, and I got a lot of laughs to and from the shop. Where there is a will, there is a way.

The front of the property adjoined Kirkwood Highway. During the snow season the state, when plowing, would fill the driveway entrance with about three feet of snow. During the night it would freeze solid. It was up to the property owner to clean his entrance. Not thinking of the freeze, I started down the driveway. Seeing the entrance packed with snow, I stopped about thirty feet back. I knew it would take some force to go through the pile. I checked the highway for traffic. When I got a break, I hit the snow at about 20 miles an hour—big mistake. The van went airborne about three feet off the ground and landed on the other lane. My head was hitting the ceiling like a PING-BALL. Luckily, nothing was coming. I pulled to the opposite edge, went up, and made a U-turn. I dug that pile of snow (ice) out with a pick.

During Easter, Betty sold Mother's Day flowers. We had a big sign near the highway. I am the worst speller; I have trouble reading because the words are spelled correctly. I spelled "mouther" on the sign. Surprisingly, we got a lot of business, a lot of comments, and a lot of laughs. One lady came up the driveway, stopped with a slide, and wanted to know who was dishonoring mothers. She said, "I can't believe mouth-ers." That's the way she read it. Well, I learned to spell mother.

While running the stove store we were required to have a state license. Betty decided to rent the front portion along the highway for $1,000 to a Christmas tree dealer, plus a free tree. That was her mad money. Also, it was rented to a furniture dealer who sold from his truck. Where there is a way, Betty will make a dollar.

C. Green was our pastor at a small church in Pennsylvania. We attended church there with our grandchildren. Charles asked me to help move a family. It was just the two of us; some others moved the larger portion. We worked until lunch. At Mcdonald's, while eating, I talked about a back catch that was giving me a problem. We were leaving, and while walking across the parking lot Charles jumped on my back with his knee pressed against my spine. I thought he wanted to wrestle. With a backward pull on my shoulders, I felt a snap; I thought he had broken my back. When he slid off me, I looked around to see if anyone was watching. My back felt better. I said, "Charles what was that all about?" He said, "I practiced therapy before I became a preacher. Now I know why he is a preacher.

Gwyneth and I were in Covington for the weekend. On the way home we stopped in Charlottesville at the University of Virginia to visit Elwood, a friend who was having a problem. After a visit we headed to Route 250 North. It is a hilly road—a lot of hills and valleys. We had the lights on and were going up a hill. I could see the reflection of lights shining above the hill. I had a curious feeling. What if that vehicle was on my side? I was cautious as I reached the brow of the road. Before reaching the top, suddenly I was faced with a car on our side of the road. Gwyneth hollered, "Daddy! Daddy!" No time to think, I was afraid to cut to his side. If he cut also we would still be head-on, I gave a sharp turn to the right. The car hit the ditch facing into a red clay embankment. We thought the car was on fire; it was caused from the car lights. I opened the door, grabbing Gwyn, and we rolled out onto the ground. By that time the occupants of the other vehicle were standing by our side. He didn't correct his position; he was still on our side. They were students at the University of Virginia, living in Pennsylvania. They were apologetic about the problem they caused. We traded information. They waited until I got out of the ditch and back on the highway. Later I went to the police station with the plate number, and they gave me his home address. I contacted his dad and explained the incident, I didn't know if they were playing chicken or not.

This is a dangerous thing, more dangerous than these Hank stories.

Betty was in Tennessee staying with a granddaughter, who had a baby girl. Therressa and I were going down to pick Betty up. We were going south on Route 81 toward Knoxville. We changed to Route 40 West. We drove to the end of Knoxville. The road was confusing; however, we were on Route 40. We traveled about forty miles, and I said, "Therressa, that truck stop looks like one that we passed on the way down!" We continued down a mountain, and I noticed the car was traveling faster than on the previous trip. I said, "Something doesn't look right." We went to the bottom of the mountain and saw a North Carolinasign. I said ah—, we have driven two hours north and east. I thought Therressa was going to throw me out of the car and continue alone. This was the dumbest thing I had ever done. I didn't even notice the north and east sign. Back on the right direction, we went for hours. Therressa was still mad as we reached our destination. We had a visit, picked up Betty, and on the way home Therressa said, "I will never travel with you again." After some time we made peace.

While splitting wood for the stove I was near the patio. I hit the wood with a glancing blow, hitting my big toe and breaking the patio door. Man, I can't win for losing—the doctor bill for my big toe and $50 to replace the glass. Betty, being conservative, bought a complete patio door for $15, I replaced it, and all was well except my big toe.

If there is no bad luck, there is no luck at all. I drove to the hunting camp on the side of a mountain near Mountain Grove. It is one-hundred-plus acres surrounded by national forest. It is really rustic; it accommodates twelve guests (hunters). After the hunt I decided to clean up around the camp. I was cutting small locust brush. Jack and others were standing around my truck discussing guns. Jack knows guns and is usually safe to be around. All at once I heard a blast. Jack had set the trigger too light on the pull, and his gun went off, hitting the truck and stopping in the other door after going through the back of the seat. I looked up in shock. I said, "Who fired that gun?" All was silent for a while, then Jack owned up. While speaking, the gun went off again. I like to—. "Jack, you could kill someone," I said. Jack couldn't figure out what was happening. When he took the safety off to unload the gun, it went off. I know how he felt.

Hunting season was open for deer using the musket. We took a vacation and drove to Covington. The children were happy; they could visit their friends. Betty could spend time with her family. It is always good to be home with Mom and Dad. Dad has eight acres behind the house on the mountain next to the national forest. I love hunting this area; I have hunted it since a boy. In the national forest are ridges, flats, and hollows. My favorite places are the ridges leading into the hollow. I had a favorite leaning dead chestnut, which I could snake up, and my scent would be off the ground. Also, it allows a clear view of the surrounding area. This tree stand is in a cross section of deer paths leading from the ridges, hollows, and flats. It is a perfect location when deer are traveling, especially mornings and evenings or in the rutting season. I hunted that morning without success.

That afternoon I returned to the same spot. It is about a two-mile walk. Arriving at the location, I placed deer lure in locations around the stand.

I snaked up the tree with my muzzleloader. I was there about one hour, and a small forked horn sneaked into the area and stopped. I had the gun in position. Aiming behind the shoulder, I squeezed the trigger. It was getting late, and I could see sparks within the smoke. The deer flinched, jumped a couple of leaps, turned in my direction and lay down at the base of the chestnut tree. Without trying to reload I looked around the ground for a stick or club. Seeing a two-inch stick, I thought this would do the job. I started gently sliding down the tree. The deer was lying upright, just looking from side to side. As I got closer I thought the deer would hear my heart beating; it sounded like a drum. As I slid closer, the deer paid no attention to me. It continued looking in the direction from which it came. I reached over, clinching the club. I drew back to hit the deer on the head, and on my forward motion the club broke off in my hand. At this, the deer staggered, getting on its feet. I dropped the rifle; all I could see was its tail. I grabbed hold of the tail. It like to broke my shoulder as it lunged forward, jerking me off the tree. Down the mountain we went, trees flashing by my head. I was making ten-foot steps. It was picking up speed. I was really stretched out, my feet hitting the ground every five steps. It was headed down a deer path toward the hollow. I was going to get killed if I hung on. Seeing a tree on my left, I decided to jump to the left when his back legs were off the ground. It worked. I threw him, and he fell against the tree. With my momentum I went about ten feet beyond the tree. I hurried back, jumped on his head with both feet, grabbed a pine knot, and worked his head over. The fall against the tree must have broken his back, it was working its front legs only. I field dressed the deer and started dragging it toward the house. On the way down I missed my glasses. I skinned the deer and placed it in the freezer. The next morning I went back to the location, hoping to have a more reasonable day and also find my glasses. Can you imagine a man holding on to a deer running 25 miles an hour?

After a hard walk I reached the area where I field dressed the deer; the intestines were still intact. I looked around for my glasses. Without finding them, I went back to the intestines, turning them with a stick. There the glasses were. I left the area and hunted toward the house.

This is not a typical deer hunt; however, when all things fail, use this method.

On another hunt, we have a camp in Interval, on the Jackson River. While there we were seeing deer. I noticed a deer path going to the river through W. Dresser's property; I contacted him at his dealership, and he gave me permission to hunt. I went down to his property, climbed a tree, and placed a board for standing. Bow season was in. It was late afternoon. I rode the four-wheeler down and parked it close to the river. I put a string on the bow, and up the tree I went. When in position I pulled up the bow. I was facing the area where the deer came through. After some time I saw squirrels, fox, beavers, and geese. As it got later and everything quieted down, I heard a rustle in that direction. Three deer came into view. I pulled my bow back on the larger doe and released, hitting the deer in the flank behind the shoulder. I waited awhile before checking the blood trail. I followed the blood trail and found the deer near an embankment below the entrance road. I went back to the four-wheeler and rode it to the deer location. After field dressing the deer, I placed it on the front rack of the 4x4. Instead of backtracking to the camp, I decided to challenge the bank—big mistake. If only I had gone twenty-five yards down, I would have hit a road. I tried going up the bank, but it was too steep. The 4x4 flipped, and backward we went. That flipped the deer on top of me. I recovered, unhurt. I loaded the deer and took a sensible way home. I mowed the river area for Mr. W. D. for his generosity.

Buddy (Harold), who worked with me, had two sons—Harold Jr. and Hank (my namesake). It was Saturday, and we decided to drive down to Assateague, Maryland. Buddy let the tires down on his Volkswagen for better traction on the sandy dunes. We went to the national end of the island. It was a more primitive part, no campsites or bath houses. At the ocean edge we discovered the skeleton hull of a sunken ship. All that was left was the framework. From there we drove to the sound side of the bay. There was plenty of wildlife to keep our interest. The ponies were the highlight of the island. The excess ponies were rounded up once a year and crossed from the island to Chincoteague, where they were sold. The income was given to the fire department. Also, we saw whitetail deer and sika deer (they are smaller, with spots). Geese were abundant on the bay side. We went into the shallow waters barefooted in order to feel for clams hidden under the mud. After the boys caught enough clams, we were prepared to boil clams. They were a little big and probably tough. We placed them in a pan over a burning flame. Having no luck at all, the gas flame burned empty. Here we were with no extra gas cylinders and partly cooked clams. We decided to build a fire and continue cooking—big mistake. While scrounging up wood, I got a dead root of poison oak and put it on the fire. It put off smoke as if it was a forest fire. Thinking only about the clams, and sometimes rubbing our eyes, we were waiting for the chef's special. Well, we would have needed a flamethrower to tenderize those clams. The made good chewing gum, if you like fishy instead of mint. We had a good outing until our eyes began to swell; that poison ivy settled all over us. Gases released from the fire like to eat us up. I felt sorry for Hank and Harold Jr. On the way home we had a scratching party. Buddy took the boys to the doctor. I used an old-fashioned remedy, homemade lye soap. Lesson learned: take your firewood with you on a camping outing. Needless to say, the boys took my fire privileges. Returning to our job on Monday, Buddy and I were both flush in the face. Our comments were that we were fighting a fire (the truth).

When I went to computer classes for the cad cam system (a method of drafting on the computer), I had the least experience on the computer. Trying to put in extra hours of learning, I would go in two hours earlier. This worked out well for some time. Somehow they changed the password. That was okay until on one early venture the password didn't work. After trying three times, the computer shut down (dead). Well, that ended my two-hour early venture. From then on I came in on time and left on time. Computers are great if you understand their procedures. Finally, I was A1. I don't know how I got along without a computer. I mastered my job, and it is so simple when using the cad cam system. I was typing rather than drafting.

In all of my design accomplishments, I received fifty-plus patents for Westvaco. I also received fifteen design awards from Paperboard Packaging Cancel.

I enjoyed my job until I became responsible for doing all design work—not just seeing that it got done by others. I was told by a supervisor that he didn't care who did it as long as it got done. This gave me an incentive to retire after 42.5 years of service. I had three great supervisors: L. Laufrenier, G. Breylinger, and C. Pittard. I found out that being friendly with your supervisor can get you out of a lot of work. I guess that's why I worked my butt off. Part of my design ability was due to a supervisor named C. Stumpp (pd). He would ask me how I intended to do a job. After explaining my method he would say, "If that doesn't work, try this." This was encouragement for me. It helped me with my creative ability. Another great supervisor was B. Bloom (e.p.m.) he gave reward for good works. (like promotions)

While living on 7.5 acres at Kirkwood Highway, we were able to have chickens, rabbits, and a goat named Fanny. She loved tobacco and would do tricks like turning flips. I began liking Delaware after moving to this location.

We have a big rooster (a Rhode Island Red). That was the meanest rooster I have ever encountered. He didn't like himself. He was a fighter; he even chased and spurred the dog. He loved it when you had your backside to him; the back of your head meant attack. You could kick him ten feet, and he would come running back. I warned everyone when coming around, always look him in the eye, stare him down. I had a cousin named Tootie (Ernest). He thought he could make friends with that rooster. He would spend time feeding him, close enough to eat out of his hand. That old bird was checking him out. Someone called Tootie, and he turned his head. That old rooster flogged his hand and all the way up his arm. He cleaned it up and, due to swelling, went to the doctor. Tootie said, "Hankie you ought to kill that rooster." I told Tootie that I warned him that old rooster was just biding his time.

One day Betty and I were working around the gardens, Betty said, "Why don't you put eight-inch stovepipes on your legs, and see what the rooster will do."

I got two stovepipes with a single wrap of corrugated, making them look like khaki pants. I took my shoes off and slipped into those pipes. Betty put my shoes back on. I walked stiff-legged around that rooster, staring him down. When I turned my back, he pounced on me. That stovepipe sounded like a cow bell; he was working the pipes over. I moved back and forth, and he thought he had me going. He flogged me so long he got tired. As he sank down by my feet, no energy left, he just pecked my feet. That old rooster was played out; he had met his match.

Days later I would see him in the yard. As I went by him I started walking stiff-legged; he took no chances. He was out of there. I didn't break him but slowed him down. He is now slow to attack, and not so brave.

My cousin (Clara) from Virginia was visiting. It was late in the afternoon, and we were having a swim at the pool. I noticed bats flying around catching bugs. We had a cookout before retiring. Clara's bedroom was on the opposite end of the house; our bedroom was near the kitchen. We retired, watching TV. After about thirty minutes a bat appeared, flying in a circle around the room. The first thing I noticed was a reflection from the bat on the wall when passing by the TV. Wow, that looked as big as a crow. We were hollering as the bat dived at our heads. I got up ducking and picked up a broom. Standing in bed, I was swinging. Betty was squealing on each pass. This went on for about fifteen minutes. Finally I swatted it, and bats are really small. We lay back down and retired. The next morning we were having coffee, and Clara said, "I would have liked to have a video of last night's orgy." I said, "No, that was a bat in our bedroom." She replied, "Sure."

I was remodeling an area of the bedroom and dining area. I purchased lumber from a nearby company. As I was sawing the proper trim length, the saw would go halfway through, and then it would split to the end of the board. This I didn't understand. I only bought what was needed; now I was short a board. I took another measurement and marked the board. I began sawing again, and the same thing happened. I was a little upset at this. I loaded up the cut and uncut boards and returned them to the store. I explained and showed them a sample of my complaint (problem). The reply was, "We don't refund on cut lumber." I replied, "I didn't have a problem until I made the cut. It only cut halfway through, then it split." He said, "That's your problem." I said, have your manager come to the front. I backed the truck to the door. The manager arrived. I said, "Would you please hold the door for me?" He said, "You don't have a cart." I said, "I don't need one." A couple of customers were in the doorway, and I ask them to move. Picking that lumber up like a spear, I threw it about forty yards down the aisle. I unloaded. The manager said, "You can't do that." I said, "I just did. If you need an explanation, talk to your clerk." I didn't get a return; however, I got my money's worth.

When walking along the stream I noticed a yellow jacket hole in the ground. They were furious, and I didn't even molest them; they were just mean. I waited until almost sunset and took another look. Most of them were in the ground. I got a plastic bucket of gasoline and poured about two gallons on and around the hole. I walked back about twenty-five yards, set the bucket down, and went within throwing distance of a match. I lit the gasoline; at that point everything around me exploded. Gas vapor around me went back, and the bucket caught fire. Well, I had $100 singe haircut, eyebrows also. It only lasted for a second, but it seemed forever. Boy, this is a fast way to get rid of yellow jackets and singe the lawn at the same time. Another lesson learned: use kerosene.

There was bad news for our rooster. The chickens roosted in a row of thirty-foot spruce trees. One night we were in bed just dozing off when we heard something above the house that sounded like a helicopter. I could hear a hair-raising squall. We had an owl on the property; he was big. That owl caught the rooster off the roost and carried him over the house. That was the last we saw of him. Yes, we miss him.

We had twenty-two chickens. One night something killed ten of them, but didn't eat them at all. That night I sat up, waiting to see the villain. Later, I heard the chickens squawking. I hesitated for a while and then got the .22 rifle and sneaked out the door to the chicken pen. A large wolf-like dog was killing the last chicken. I opened up the .22 and emptied it. I wasn't sure about the animal. It had no collar.

CHAPTER VI

Retirement Adventure

W HEN WE MOVED to Delaware I borrowed $2,000 from dad, I paid him back with Westvaco stock. I retired from westvaco in 1992 at the age of 62 after 42.5 years of service. Betty and I decided to return to virginia. We advertised our property of 7.5 acres with home and four grages for sale; a builder said he would purchase the property if he could multiple zoning. The zoning was approved after three months. The selling price was $635,000, we had a fixed income through westvaco savings of 16% of my salary plus westvaco gave an additional 6% as an incentive, plus they gave a retirement benefit. Westvaco is a great family oriented company, they were interested in your future.

The builder had a total of fifty townhouses on the property, we held part of the purchase price at 5% intrest, this gave us additional income.

Betty contracted the furniture dealer who set up on the front property to move us to Virginia when he went south to pick up furniture.

We loaded the loaded the motor home and went to our newly purchased 13 room home called the Hockman house. Betty started a bed and breakfast. The house was on 6.1 acres on the north fork of the shanadoah river in edinburg off route 81 and 11. The purchase price was $235,000. Remember you cant out give god.

Additional Hank stories will continue at this Hockman House location.

We met the movers at the Hockman House. Our help was Alfred (brother-in-law), a furniture man; Durwood (Realtor); myself and Betty. Betty was the coordinator. As we carried the furniture in, Betty pointed the location. It was quite a challenge, with many steps involved. By the day's end, Betty had the house organized. We got the furniture hauled at a reasonable price; he was deadheading back to North Carolina for another load.

We were tired after unloading and went to bed for a good night's rest.

The next day I made a list of improvements to be made in the yard area, mainly trimming shrubbery and taking out brush, along with overgrowth on the hill leading to the river. Betty had a dream of a courtyard; she sketched it out, and I installed it to her recommendation. The yard work took weeks. I had a beautiful sign made by Sergio of Delaware for the Hockman House bed and breakfast.

After the grounds were finished, Betty wanted the house painted—gray on the bricks, maroon on the trim and metal roof. Garry was the paint contractor.

While it was being painted, I made dental, (various size blocks) to form the top trim. After all this work I was ready for a break.

Betty and I went to the flea market just for a fun day. Betty looked around for antiques, and I searched for guns. Betty bought a walnut chest of drawers with side locks and a blanket chest. On the way out we saw three miniature goats, two nannies and a bad billy. We thought this would be good for the four acres that was brushy. We purchased the goats and headed for home; we put collars on the two girl goats without any problem; that billy was another case. Trying to collar him, he got under the van. For a little fellow he was strong. I thought he was going to tear the muffler off.

Finally he came out, and I got a collar and chain on him. We kept them on a chain, moving them from location to location to eat the undergrowth. Later we put in an electric fence.

While the Goats (girls) were small we trained them to be car broke, we would take them on trips when traveling. On one trip to Delaware to show the girls to our daughter Therrissa we stopped at a Cheverolet dealer to check out a new vehicle. We were in the office the girls (goats) were in the van. It ws a bright hot sunny day and I said the Girls are probably hot in that van. The Sailsman said bring the Girls in. The sales force had a surprise look when they saw me lead in those two goats. The goats needed to relieve thimself (go to the bathroom) they saw that nice green carpet and both of them cut loose. It looked like a pellet factory, a continuous digester. One of the sales group picked up a broom with dust pan and cleaned up after the girls, needless to say we didn't discuss car sales after that. That is one way to get even with a car salesman (payback).

When preparing for the bed and breakfast I started on the interior remodeling; the upstairs game room, it was twenty by forty feet. I enclosed one corner and made a walk-in closet; on the opposite side I made a bar with a sink and small under-counter refrigerator. I used wainscot to match the décor. Facing the river were double doors and a twenty by twenty deck.

Next I started on a bath for every room; the rooms were sixteen by sixteen. I placed the baths in the corners, using corner showers. Wainscot was installed on the bottom three feet. I used one-foot mirrow squares to finish the walls before installing the light. I called the air condition service and asked if the current going to the AC was 120 or 220. He said 120. I put in the lights and hooked them up. I flipped the switch and, wow, what a light. I said to Betty, "You don't need but one bulb to light this area." As we were commenting on the brightness, there was a series of pops. Every bulb exploded. That was no 120 current; I hooked into the 220. Don't believe everything you hear, even if it is from a pro. I rewired, and it wasn't so bright.

The kitchen was the same size as the game room. I installed an insert in the fireplace (every room had a fireplace). I purchased custom replacement windows. The picture window was made in three parts, I was installing them from the interior. With the windows out, I (alone) picked up the large center window and positioned it in the opening. The wind blew and caught the window, pulling it through the opening. Luckily for me, Betty was nearby. I was holding on to the window as it was falling through the opening. I was going out with it, too dumb to let go. Betty, seeing what was happening, caught me by the belt and held on with both hands. I was partly outside; she prevented me from falling. I was glad she wasn't angry at me. She saved me and the window.

We mowed two acres, some of which was a hill from the house to the river, about two hundred yards. The hill was steeper on one side than the other. I tried mowing down the steep side, and the tractor would go out of control—no friction on the back wheels; they seemed to skip and turn backward. I wised up and mowed down the less steep and up the steep side. This worked out well. I also mowed from side to side; the problem with this was that I slid off the seat toward the down side.

On one occasion I was mowing the flat area near the river. I was close to the river edge, and the front wheel hit a stump and slid the front end of the mower over the edge. When I tried backing up, the tires spun. One of the back tires was hardly on the ground, no traction. Afraid the mower was going to slide in the river, I got off and tried pulling it back—big mistake. As I pulled back, the front end slid sideways, starting into the river.

Here I was on the rear end of a mower starting to slide into the river, my feet loosing grip and sliding with the mower. This was worse than tailing a deer; the engine was still running. I didn't have a free hand to cut the ignition. Slowly, inch by inch, I was losing the mower, still holding on; the front end began to sink. The muffler started blowing bubbles, the engine still running. It began to put off a cloud of smoke as the engine went under. You couldn't see the opposite side for the smoke. I let go when I knew I had lost the battle. I just looked around to see if anyone was watching because of the smoke. Sheepishly, I went to the house and explained the episode to Betty. She just shook her head. My grandson was there, and I asked if he would help pull the mower out of the river. With a smile on his face he agreed. We drove to the river. When Mat saw the tractor setting in the river, he couldn't contain himself. He rolled into a big, continuous laugh. After seeing the situation, we hooked a chain to the tractor, and I gently brought the tractor up the bank and back to level ground. I really drowned that mower. I pulled the tractor back to the house and began to flush the engine, replacing the oil. Luckily, the engine started. I only ran it for a minute and then drained the mixed oil and water out; it looked like chocolate milk. I did this three times before the drainage looked like oil. That was a tough tractor; it ran for many seasons.

Another day when mowing at the river I stayed a foot away from the edge. As I finished that area, I thought I would go up the steep side. It was a greater degree of steepness. As I started up the bank I began to feel the front of the tractor rise; I tried standing and leaning over the hood to hold it down. The tractor flipped backward. I fell back, and the tractor landed on the seat, still running. It looked like a helicopter with those blades turning. I raised one leg, put my foot against the seat, and gave a big shove; the tractor turned over, and the engine shut down.

Well, after this episode I decided to get the tractor serviced. With the ramps in place I went forward and up, the mower deck hitting the truck bed, throwing it sideways, and, yes, off I went about ten feet over, landing on the pavement. Man, I just can't win for losing. I am not that hazardous; crap just happens.

Trying to change my luck, I decided to go fishing. I called Bryant (grandson) and asked if he would like to go below the dam fishing. We got in the canoe, and to the dam we went. The fishing was better below the dam because of the oxidation of the fallen water. I put the boat into the bank. There is an old saying, "Don't do as I do, but do as I tell you to do." Before leaving the canoe I said to Bryant, "Don't get out on the side; step out the front of the canoe." He did it perfectly and was sitting down when over the side I went like an out-of-control frog. I went under in a circular motion. I didn't know which end was up. I had vertigo, and it seemed forever before I came up. Bryant was sitting with his budged cheeks looking like a ground squirrel; he wanted to laugh but didn't. I said, "Bryant, go on over to the other side. I will follow you a little later." I could hear him cracking up. After getting my head together, I joined him at the bottom of the dam. We had good laughs as each had a good day fishing. As usual, Bryant caught a nice smallmouth bass.

My nephew Bobby made me another pair of glasses. When delivering them he had a bobber float on each side. That was a hard one to live down.

My worst day. We had a garden about one hundred yards from the house. I watered it with a hose when it was dry. It was good, fertile ground and produced a good yield of various plants.

The grass needed mowing. As I started the tractor I noticed a flat front tire. In order to remove the wheel and tire, I placed a gallon paint can under the axle for support. At the same period I treated my dog with dust for his fleas. Usually I used SEVEN dust; however, being out of Sevin, I substituted Dragon dust (not knowing it was toxic).

I returned to the mower and fixed the flat. Another senior moment, I started the tractor; the cutting blades were engaged and twirling. When going forward, I forgot to move the paint can. Man, what a mess. All around it looked like a slaughterhouse, red paint everywhere. I knew the paint should be washed off before drying. I raced to the garden to retrieve the water hose. Passing by my dog, I notice him in convulsion. He previously was licking the dust. I didn't know whether to wash off the red paint or tend to the dog. I called Betty for some support. I went to the dog, trying to revive him. I sprinkled him down with water and pressed on his chest—nothing. He was dead, and I said to Betty, "I killed my dog." Betty said, "Where did the blood come from? Are you hurt?" "No," I said. "Oh, crap. I forgot about the paint." I dragged the hose to the tractor and hosed both the building and the tractor down. It came off the building; however, I had a polka-dot tractor.

Betty made brandied fruit. It was started with vodka to give it a boost; the fruit additives were unsweetened. It turned out to be a thick, syrupy solution. The fruit was crunchy; it was delicious on ice cream. About a quart was in the refrigerator for over a year. I put it in a bowl with a little water, mixed it, and placed it outside beside the dog feeder. We were watching out the picture window. The dog came by and started eating the fruit; he was really lapping it up. After a few minutes he would just stare at the fruit bowl, and then he would go forward, with his nose hitting the ground. He stood there a little wobbly and began eating again. This time when he went forward his front legs buckled, and down he went on his shoulders. Finally he wobbled up and began to walk with a stagger; he fell from side to side before taking a nap under a spruce tree. I didn't realize this fruit was that strong. Well, he was a happy dozer; he slept for hours.

Bad billy was acting up; we couldn't keep him on the chain. He constantly tangled up the girl goats' chains. I placed their houses in a small area with an electric fence surrounding them. Billy was curious about that wire; as I watched he decided to check out the wire. He got within three inches of the wire and began to sniff. Smelling nothing, he decided to lick the wire. When his tongue hit the wire, I thought his eyes were going to explode. They increased in size as he began turning flips and jumping sideways. After he settled down he went over and butted the girl goats. He was a smart bad billy. He learned to crawl under the wire; the hair on his back insulated him from the effects of the wire. He was constantly out of the pen. When I yelled at him he would jump the wire back into the pen. He stayed close because the girl goats were confined to the pen.

I was repairing the upstairs bathroom faucet. While removing the valve I dropped a nut into the washer area. I ask Gwyn to go down to the main faucet and turn it on slowly, hoping the pressure would flush up the nut. It would raise about one-half inch, as if to float. I yelled to increase the flow—big mistake. She must have turned it wide open; the nut flew out, bouncing off my head. I was yelling, "Cut it off." All I could hear was, "What? What did you say, Daddy?" Well, before cutting the water off, the bath had one-half inch of water in the floor. Finally Gwyn came up to see what the excitement was about. With a grin she pulled a Zerkial: "Did I do that?" My reply was, "Yes, and you are going to clean it up." In a situation like this you need two phones or walkie-talkies for communication.

We were planning on painting the woodwork maroon. That would look good with the gray bricks. I set up a ladder, tied it off, and started the pressure washer. Up I went about thirty feet. I was standing firm and holding on with one hand. When I started the spray washer the pressure kicked me back, and I lost footing on the ladder. The sprayer wand was moving back and forth; I couldn't release the trigger. It continued dancing me around on the ladder, with one arm holding on. Finally someone on the ground, seeing my problem, cut the engine off. Man, they saved my life. My arm must have stretched an inch; it was sore for a week.

We learn from our mistakes. I have done a lot of learning.

We had a conversion van we used for trips; I was ready to sell it. I sold it to a church member. To make sure it was in good condition I planned on having the garage check it out.

Previously I was complaining to Betty about double parking in the driveway. In other words, don't block the driveway. Being a good wife, she parked behind the van. Unaware the car was behind the van, I backed up without looking. Suddenly there was a crash. Great, both vehicles were damaged. The estimate for the van repairs was $500. I said to Ken, "I'm not repairing the van. If you still want it, you can deduct $500 from the price I gave you." He was happy with the deal, and so was I.

We had a great experience running the bed and breakfast. We met a large number of interesting people, including the Hockman families.

Betty had two auctions selling furniture not needed for the next house; also she sold a great number of antiques and McCoy pottery. The total sales, including junk, amounted to $80,000; she was often teased of getting this much for her junk.

We planned on moving closer to Betty's aging mother.

We found a beautiful antebellum home with large front porch pillars reaching through the second floor. Prior to moving in we decided to repair the much needed work.

Mainly cosmetic—painting the exterior, new wood in areas of the porch, and trim banisters around the upper level. The interior floors were sanded and refinished; the library was papered, and the kitchen was enlarged by removing one wall, making it double in size. New chandeliers and upgraded wiring were added, along with new replacement windows. I put in a bath with a walk-up shower on the tub; this was added to the master bedroom. It was a lot of work; it was done with a lot of stories.

While repairing the porch, which was U shaped, I fell through one of the decayed boards and broke a rib. This is no laughing matter; the more you laugh, the harder it hurts. I took shallow breaths for about three weeks.

My next encounter was in the master bath. While prying up hardwood oak flooring to install water lines, I had a wrecking bar lifting up one end of the board. I placed my fingers under the board in order to lift up on it. At that instant the pry bar slipped and pinched three of my fingers. Here I was, caught by a board monster holding me by three fingers. I finally placed the pry bar under the board to relieve my fingers, not quite broken but severely skinned and dented. It was my left hand, so I was still in business.

The basement door was on the laundry room floor. It was a trapdoor hinged on one side; it could be lifted and swung to the wall and attached. As I was working in this area, I secured the door in the open position while working on the steps below. The door wasn't that securely latched; the door came down with a crash, pinning my head between the door and the steps. I was seeing stars and felt faintly no one was around when you need help. Finally, with my shoulder against the door, I was able to wiggle my head out. I just had my head skinned on two sides and a sore jaw—nothing serious. I was still able to work.

A narrow escape was when I was putting siding up about thirty feet on a closet over a side porch. I was within three feet of the edge, and the ladder began to slide. One side of the ladder went off the corner of the construction. Here I was, knees shaking, and the ladder tilting with every shake. I thought I had had it—too afraid to move downward and unable to stabilize the ladder. No one was around, and the ladder wasn't tied off. I jumped the ladder and leaned to my left; it moved about two inches. Repeating this several times, the ladder was back in position. Before going back up the ladder, I tied it off at top and bottom. The repairs completed we were ready to move.

When we decided to move I bought a $300 trailer, which was a modification of a pop-up camper. I installed eight-foot two-by-fours on each corner to get additional height. I used strips to enclose the sides. This was used for hauling banana boxes filled with clothing, glassware, and other small articles. We rented a U-Haul for the furnishings.

Pat, our cousin, was on the valley police force. He had a day off and volunteered to help with a load to Clifton Forge. The banana boxes were donated by Food Lion; they were sturdy and can be used for safely transporting items. We had the trailer packed within one foot of the top rails, similar to *The Beverly Hillbillies*. We were going about 65 miles an hour, when a tractor trailer blew the horn several times. Pat (the officer/cop) said, "Hank, I think that truck wants to pass. He is letting you know to stay in your lane, not the passing lane. That's why he is continuously on the horn." Well, big surprise, when that tractor trailer went by me blasting his horn, I was about to lose control. Looking up as he passed, the lid of one of the banana boxes was hanging on his mirror. Pat said, "Hank, legally that can get you in trouble." I was glad he was riding with me and not in a squad car. The lid was all we lost; the banana box lid remained on the mirror as he went out of sight. I reduced speed in order not to catch up. Needless to say, I got a lesson on packing securely, and safely.

We continue to use the trailer in other ways.

With this $300 trailer, I went to Back Creek Mountain, where our hunting camp is located, to cut a load of wood, for the wood burning insert we installed, I replaced the trailer tires.

When tightening the lugs to ensure a trouble-free load, I didn't have the proper wrench. As I was cutting down a tree, the saw was pinched. Luckily, I had an extra saw. I used it, trying to free the pinched saw. My luck was kicking in; the tree fell, but instead of freeing the saw, it cracked the housing. This is going to be an expensive load of wood. I cut enough wood to fill the trailer and the truck bed. When positioning the truck to hook up the trailer, I got on a soft area of the hill, and the truck slid against a tree. Wow, I couldn't pull up or back up. The tree was within inches of the back tire. I placed a wedge between the tire and the tree to ensure the tree falling away from the truck. I also placed a rope on the tree about ten feet up and tied it off to another tree about fifteen feet away. I didn't want to take a chance on the tree falling on the truck bed. I notched the tree in the fall direction and went above the notch about one foot and cautiously started an angular cut toward the notch. This was working okay. As the saw cut closer to the notch, the tree began to crack and fall in a direction away from the truck. This was luck, or maybe someone was looking out for me. Finally the tree was on the ground; it fell in the path going to the spring. I decided to let the next person using the spring cut the tree away; I didn't want to take a chance on pinching another saw. We hooked up the trailer and started the three-mile trip to the main road. Going down, I encountered a lot of bouncing; the trailer was hooked to a ball on the bumper. I checked the bumper, and it was tilting down from the bouncing. I also checked the tires; the wheels were getting loose because the lugs were not tight enough. This was turning out to be a nightmare, only one-quarter mile to the highway. When reaching the highway I was done. Wheels loose and the bumper falling off, I drove very cautiously until reaching a parking area about a mile away. I unhooked the trailer and left it setting until I returned with a different truck. By the time I got the wood home, I think it cost me $500 a cord.

On another wood-cutting event I used my new truck. The trailer wheels were repaired and ready for hauling. I filled both the trailer and the truck, no problems. With the new truck pulling the trailer, you hardly knew it was in tow. Everything was going great. When reaching home, I pulled to the street above in order to turn around. In a senior moment, I forgot the trailer behind me. Backing up, the trailer jackknifed and caved the side of the truck bed in. Needless to say what this load cost. At this I changed to a gas log fireplace.

My truck was a Chevrolet crew cab and was fairly new. I went to the Ford garage, no intention of selling or trading. I parked beside the main door entrance. When entering the showroom the manager approached me, wanting to check out my truck. I thought nothing about it, or about what his motive was. I think he wanted me to trade. When he returned, he parked the truck near the front door and the sidewalk. He talked of what he would give me on a trade; I wasn't interested. The truck was only six months old. It was a nice day, and other salesmen were outside near the truck. I spoke to them and got in the truck and started to drive off to the right. All at once I heard a crushing of metal and salesmen hollering. That jerk parked my truck beside a fire hydrant. I didn't see it, and when pulling off I tore the door almost off. I got out jumping and yelling, "What idiot parked my truck beside that hydrant?" I had a $500 deductible. They paid part—no longer a customer.

The side porches needed new roofing; I decided to use metal instead of slate.

The roof was about thirty feet from the ground. I placed the ladder in position and tied it off, and I placed the needed materials on one end and started positioning and nailing the sheets in place. The sheets extended fifteen inches over the roof; I planned on installing the entire roof and then chalk line a two-inch overhang and make all the cuts in one motion. This would make a straight-line cut. I worked into an area where the drain line came from the upper roof. The area needed cuts to accommodate the drain pipe. I turned and accidentally stepped on the overhang. It was like a sled; as it bent down I shot off the roof. Face up and back down, it was like a swimmer doing the backstroke. I just closed my eyes and waited for the thump; it seemed like forever hitting the ground. The fall wasn't that bad; it was the sudden stop. When I came to, I was trying to remember what I was doing lying on the ground. I wiggled my toes, checking out movement. I then lifted each foot; the sudden stop threw the shoes off my feet. Betty heard me fall and called emergency. They brought a doctor with them. Checking me out, they cut both legs of my trousers to the waist. They strapped me to a stretcher and transported me to the hospital; they x-rayed me from head to toe. After finding no breaks, they again checked my vitals and made sure I had body functions before releasing me.

Betty refused to let me back on the roof. I waited until she left the house and went up and finished the job. If you fall off a horse, you get back on.

After this ordeal I decided to float the Jackson River and fish. I called Alfred, my brother-in-law, to go with me. I had a small bass boat. We put in at Indian Draft and planned on fishing to Petticoat Junction. We caught several nice trout. We were going down a riffle. At the end, about fifty yards, was a nice deep hole. The plan was to put out the anchor about ten feet from the hole (pool). I threw the anchor out the back of the boat. The current was too swift; it carried us into the front of the pool, and the anchor caught. We came to a sudden stop; at that point the fast water came into the boat. We were standing knee deep in the middle of the hole of water, and the anchor was holding us in that position. The boat was double wall and couldn't sink. The problem was that we couldn't move. I got out of the back of the boat to free the anchor, and water completely filled the boat. Alfred caught an overhanging branch and pulled the boat to the water's edge. Here we were, with three hundred gallons of water in a sinking boat; we had a hard time edging the boat to the side and trying to lift up one side and empty the water. Inch by inch we finally lifted to an angle where all of the water was on the opposite side of the boat, this worked in our favor. We finally pulled the boat to dry ground and turned it over. Luckily, we didn't lose anything. We placed the boat back in the river, and away we went. We did very little fishing on the way down. Lesson learned: go to the bank before encountering swift water, and don't throw an anchor out of the back of a boat.

When I got home we cleaned the fish, and Alfred was glad to leave my presence. I decided to stay out of trouble. I went up to the gun room. I remembered I left cartridges in the .260 rifle. I wiped the gun down and ejected the shells (I thought). I checked the chamber, and it was clear. I rebolted the chamber and placed the safety on. (Or did I?) I squeezed the trigger, and everything hit the fan. Wow, what an explosion in small quarters. The bullet hit a metal radiator; it was like a war zone, with metal and water flying in all directions. Betty came up the steps panicky; I was so shook up I didn't know where to turn—one-half inch of water on the floor and running strong. Betty said, "Go downstairs and cut the water off." She called the plumber Swope.

For the first time, he responded quickly. He took the damaged radiator out and blocked it off.

Betty got real smart and brave. She put a set of deer antlers on the radiator, took a picture, and said, "Hank's latest kill."

The radiator set on the porch for a while as a reminder of how dumb you can be. Never trust an empty gun; they will hurt you or do damage.

I ordered a new tree stand. It was called a tree lounge; it sounded great, reclining up a tre

Delivered it one afternoon about two o'clock, I checked the components parts without reading any instructions. I headed for my favorite place in the mountains.

I picked out a tree on the side of the ridge; it had a good slope, and deer trails were on both sides of the tree. I laid out the stand base first and hinged the bar around the tree, locking it into position. I placed the lounge section above and locked it with the same feature. It worked by lifting up on the back part of the lounge; at the same time you lifted the front area around the tree up. The base was similar; it had a strap for lifting up with your feet. Releasable, it attached to your boot; this created a climbing effect similar to a jack. The advertising showed it attached to a six-inch tree; I had it attached to a larger-diameter tree. This gave me a lesser angle, also allowing less lift in the rear, allowing raising or lowering. I was up about twenty-five feet. When climbing you face the tree; then you turn in the opposite direction. Before turning, I fastened the safety harness to the stand and the tree. When turning I lifted my leg over the lounge area, and my boot lifted the back of the lounge to about 90 degrees. It lost friction on the tree and fell to the base section. The weight of the fall caused the base to lose friction, and down we went. The stand fell within three feet of the ground and stopped with a sudden jerk. I went down with it, and when it stopped it threw me out upside down and swinging like a pendulum. The safety belt did its job. There I was, hanging upside down swinging back and forth, my nose hitting the ground and my head hitting the tree. It sounded like a woodpecker barking a tree. It took me forever to loosen the safety belt. When it came loose, I went down the ridge about fifteen feet on my head and shoulder. I lay there until I came to my senses, and then I started back up to the stand location. I was missing my glasses. No need trying to hunt this area; the fall scared all animals off this ridge.

The next day I returned to the area, within twenty-five feet of my fall. I started raking the leaves looking for my glasses. I found them about five feet from the fall area.

The stand had a manufacturing design defect; the part around the tree had no biting effect, allowing it to lose friction under such circumstances. I sent an improved design to the company with a complaint of my fall. Later they changed the design. They didn't acknowledge wrongdoing and ignored my complaint; they didn't send me an add-on repair.

On another day I looked for a suitable tree I could climb. I found an old abandoned tree stand, mostly rotted from age. It still had climbing steps nailed to the tree. Using my gun sling, I placed it around my shoulder and started to climb. I was careful not to step on a broken step. About ten feet up the step gave way, and down I went. I was trying to hold on to the tree; the old nails were skinning up my hands. All at once, I softly hit the ground. It was if I had been gently lowered. This puzzled me; however, I didn't try that climb again. When I walked away from the tree my pants fell down. I noticed the belt was still buckled; the belt was in two pieces. It had caught on a nail, breaking my fall. Some things are hard to believe.

I am a nut when it comes to hunting off the ground. I was in a rocky area, and I noticed a nice tree with limbs suitable for climbing. At the center area was a nice fork as a backrest. It took me a while to climb and get into position; from this height I could cover lead ridges and flats. When I sat down and leaned against the fork, my momentum didn't stop. The limb broke off, and down I went into that rock pile. My gun hit the rocks first, and I landed on the gun and rocks. When I picked up the gun by the strap, the gun dangled in three pieces. The stock was broken in two places. Now I have ruined my favorite gun, a Mannlicher-Schoenauer. I guess I will never learn that what goes up must come down. I cleaned and sanded the parts and used Weldwood glue; it finished nicely, with only hairline cracks.

When working for Westvaco, I designed packaging, various items, and designs.

The trend in burials was leading to cremation. I came up with a four-piece memorial for housing a family's ashes. It consisted of a three-foot capsule extending into the ground. It had a marble base, with an aperture (diameter) the size of an urn, and a bronze memorial plate, also having an aperture. All pieces were in line with the capsule. At this point urns (ashes) can be placed through the apertures into the capsule. A bronze cover plate using four screws was placed over the entrance to the capsule; when additional ashes went into the capsule, you only removed the plate with the four screws. I received a patent on these features, patent number 6,904,721. This method also used less burial plot; you could take a standard three by nine grave site and divide it into three three-foot sections.

I purchased 360 sites, three by three, and laid out an economy burial garden. The sites were sold to me for resale. After all my labors I found out they sold me the lots illegally; I couldn't resell them. My investment was dormant for three years. Finally a federal person approached the sellers, and they refunded my investment when showing proof of receipts. Know what you are getting into before you act. My intent was to franchise the patent. Needless to say, I lost interest. I still have our burial sites in that location.

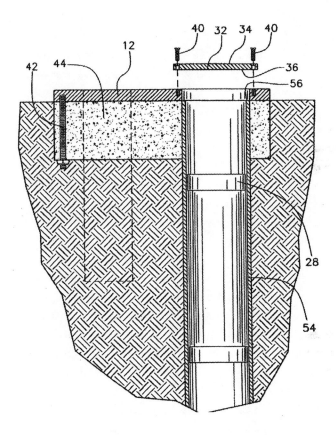

While working on the cremation garden I had a lighthouse made of marble.

Around the base I needed limestone rocks. I went to the quarry and purchased a ton of stones. They were in the trailer, and the tires were almost flat. The loader said, "You can't go far with those low tires." I had ten miles to go. Cautiously I came from the quarry to a location that had air. The tires was smoking when I arrived—a lot of friction on low tires. I made it to my destination. Don't load a ton on a half-ton trailer.

I was building a house in Riverview Estates. I went to Lowe's to purchase cinderblocks. They loaded a skid on the truck; I couldn't get the tailgate closed. There was an overhang. I drove over the mountain to the Riverview location, about fifty miles. The grade going up the mountain to the site was very steep. I placed the truck in a low gear and moved slowly up the grade. The steep grade with a slick bed liner made a slippery condition. All at once the skid slid off, breaking about half the blocks. Here I was in the middle of the road with a pile of blocks blocking the road. Panicky, I called Betty. She picked up Roger, my helper, and brought him to the area. I was working my butt off when Roger arrived. He wanted to make a joking situation over the spill. I said, "Roger, put a sock in it. I'm not in a joking mood. We cleaned the area and drove the fifty-foot distance to the work site. Another lesson learned: don't make a load where you can't close the tailgate.

Therressa and I decided to go fishing. We put the boat in at Indian Draft, that would give us a four-mile drift to Petticoat Junction. Trissa loved to fish; we were catching twelve—to fourteen-inch trout. She made a cast into swift water above a nice pool. When the spinner (rooster tail) passed into the clear water, the black and gold glittered as it spun. A big trout rolled over, and the fight was on. She landed the twenty-inch trout with the help of a net. That was the biggest of the day. I placed it on the chain with the other trout. We came to a shallow area above the rapids; the boat was dragging, and I got out and pulled it into deeper water. In the transaction, I accidentally stepped on the fish chain, breaking it off. Therressa's trophy was nowhere to be seen. When I told her the bad news, I thought she was going to leave me in the water. After a while she joked about it, saying, "You can't stand being outfished, so you turned my catch loose." She caught additional fish, but none as big as the one I released. We reached the junction and began to pull the boat up the ramp; water in the boat went to the area of my camera and got it wet.

We loaded up and started to the camp in Interval. The sky was getting dark. It started sprinkling rain, and it looked stormy. All at once there was a flash close by; it seemed just overhead. As we drove, it got worse. The lightning lit up the interior of the truck. I said, "The lightning is getting worse. It seems to be following us." It was so close that I reacted by ducking. I don't know what good that would have done. This was the worst lightning storm I have experienced. We reached the camp and began to carry out our gear. As I picked up the camera, and it began flashing. The water shorted out the camera, creating a lightning storm. Don't believe everything you see; investigate. I will never live these two incidents down.

I was working on the house I was building in Riverview Estates. I was on a ladder with hammer in hand and was swinging upward, driving a nail in. The hammer hit a glancing blow, striking me in the forehead, I didn't fall off the ladder, but my knees buckled. I know what they mean when they say they saw stars. I saw the Milky Way. I had a healthy egg in the middle of my forehead. Betty said, "Are you okay?" I said, "Just a little dizzy." Betty's reaction to that was, "You have always been dizzy." The knot went down after a while.

I was putting in the water and sewer to the house. It was a three-quarter-inch plastic line, and it was joined together with metal screw clamps. When arriving the next day, I found a separation of the line under the house, and it was running full blast. I went to the main valve and cut it off. I played innocent and called the county waterworks. They sent a man to check out the meter; it read thirty-five thousand gallons used. My comment was, "How can I use that much water?" He replied that it went through the meter. Needless to say, I had the biggest water bill ever.

If it wasn't for bad luck, I would have no luck at all. I was backing up in the snow; it was a steep area, and the truck slid into a culvert and busted a tire. I pulled to the edge, where there was a ditch running parallel down the grade. It took me forever to change the tire; it was new to me. A neighbor and his son came to my rescue; they knew what they were doing. It was starting to snow; I was parked in the ditch. I was going down the grade but was not getting on the hardtop. As I gunned the engine, the truck jumped out of the ditch into the highway. In about three complete spins, I landed up against a tree, and the front was partly over the bank. The wrecker came and cut the tree and pulled the truck to safety. I am thinking about selling that truck.

This is my ending story. It may be considered a senior moment.

I was selling my crew cab truck. It was parked at a station across from the courthouse. I drove down to clean everything out of the truck. I placed everything in the trunk of the car. Two days later I decided to drive the truck. I parked the car and drove the truck for two days. I asked Betty to drive down with me and pick up the other car. When we arrived, the car was not in the front area of the parking lot. We discussed it, and I decided it was moved or stolen. The police station was next door, and I reported the missing car. I explained that the car was parked at the location for two days. They called around to find out if a wrecking service had moved the vehicle. After taking all the information and filing the complaint, we left. I decided to drive behind the station and check out the alley. To my surprise, the car was parked in the rear of the station. I went back to the police station and told them of my find. One of the officers went to the location, and we checked the car out. It was locked. We checked the trunk, and it was okay. We couldn't understand this situation. Finally, backtracking, I remembered that the front of the lot was full, and I had parked in the back. I have lost a car in a parking garage, but never thirty feet away. At eighty-one, it's easy to lose your wheels.